PAMPHLETS ON AMERICAN WRITERS • NUMBER 73

UNIVERSITY OF MINNESOTA

↙ *Norman Mailer*

BY RICHARD FOSTER

UNIVERSITY OF MINNESOTA PRESS · MINNEAPOLIS

PUBLISHED IN GREAT BRITAIN, INDIA, AND PAKISTAN BY THE OXFORD
UNIVERSITY PRESS, LONDON, BOMBAY, AND KARACHI, AND IN CANADA
BY THE COPP CLARK PUBLISHING CO. LIMITED, TORONTO

FOR IRWIN AND WENDELL COREY

RICHARD FOSTER, a professor of English at Macalester College, is the author of *The New Romantics* and co-editor of *Modern Criticism: Theory and Practice.*

◢ *Norman Mailer*

WHEN Norman Mailer's *The Naked and the Dead* was published in 1948 it was all but universally acclaimed as a major novel marking the appearance of a new American writer destined for greatness. During the next twenty years, however, though he had some warm defenders, the negative judgments among critics substantially outnumbered the positive as book after book appeared: novels, a play, collections of stories and poems, and gatherings of essays and other fugitive pieces. And yet, unlike most of his generation of novelists — the "war novelists" and the urban Jewish writers — he has pursued a course of individualistic development and change which has continued to command the attention of peers, critics, and public; if his readers have sometimes been baffled and frequently hostile they have grown ever more interested. To use a Maileresque analogy, he has rather resembled an overmatched boxer who, floored in the second round, springs back and sustains the fight far beyond expectations through variety and inventiveness of footwork and temporizing punches.

The match is still not decided. But however it finally comes out, there can be no doubt that the overmatched boxer will at the very least be remembered for his remarkable performance. Mailer's adversary through the 1950's and 1960's has been the current embodiment of operative cultural and literary norms, that plodding but powerful opponent of idiosyncrasy and innovation which Eliot long ago dubbed "the tradition." Mailer had won his first round with a skillful and moving but conventional novel in the realist-naturalist vein. Everything since *The Naked and the Dead*,

5

with the exception of a handful of stories from the late forties and early fifties, has been radically innovative in both substance and essential form — without satisfying current conceptions of what constitutes serious literary experimentation.

It has been Mailer's apparent lack of artistic "seriousness" that has troubled his serious critics most. When they were not either ridiculing or dismissing him, their main cry was the lamentation that a major talent was being wasted on trivial material or debased by sloppy craftsmanship. F. Scott Fitzgerald, whose work and career were in many ways similar to Mailer's, was criticized during his lifetime on much the same grounds. But what needs to be stressed in Mailer's case, as in Fitzgerald's, is that he is indeed a serious "experimentalist" writer, though an experimentalist of a different order than our moment in the history of "the tradition" allows us easily to recognize, accept, and understand.

James Joyce was the kind of experimentalist who applied innovative techniques to conventionally "realistic" fictional material. He sought out and found new routes to the old novelistic destinations. D. H. Lawrence, on the other hand, was the kind of writer who discovered new destinations — new materials and knowledge, and thus new obligations for fiction. His technical innovations, always less sophisticated, formal, and predominant than Joyce's, were functional consequences and by-products of what can only be called an experimentalist approach to the *subject matter* of fiction. In the course of writing *The Rainbow* and *Women in Love*, Lawrence discovered, as he told Edward Garnett, that his subject was no longer "the old stable *ego*" of human character, no longer the "diamond" but rather the "carbon" which is the diamond's elemental substance: "There is another *ego*, according to whose action the individual is unrecognisable, and passes through, as it were, allotropic states which it needs a deeper sense than any we've been used to exercise, to discover are states of the same single radically unchanged element. . . . Again I say, don't look for the development of the novel to follow the lines of certain characters: the characters fall into the form of some other rhythmic form, as when one draws a fiddle-bow across a fine tray delicately sanded, the sand takes lines unknown."

These metaphors describing the substantive nature of Lawrence's experimentation with both matter and form after *Sons and Lovers* might as easily apply to Mailer, whose work after *The Naked and the Dead* has been similarly concerned with the "allotropy" — the changing "rhythmic form" and "lines unknown" — of the "carbon" of human character under complex stress. And like Lawrence, Mailer seems to have become aware of his new departure only after standing away from the new work in hand to see what he was doing and why he was doing it. While working on *Barbary Shore*, he has recalled in an interview, he found his Marxist intellectual convictions continually distracted by compulsive preoccupations with "murder, suicide, orgy, psychosis." "I always felt as if I were not writing the book myself." Other statements by Mailer indicate that much the same creative pathology also ruled the composition of *The Deer Park*, his third novel. The personal stresses and anxieties that underlay the writing of these two novels, and the stories that were spun off from them, found confessional expression in Mailer's fourth book, a compilation of fiction and nonfiction pieces with unifying connective additions called *Advertisements for Myself*, which is the author's intense, immediate, and unabashedly public reappraisal of himself, in 1959, as both artist and human being. Anxiety, compulsion, and hints of psychosis had been the disruptive and only half-conscious creative causes behind *Barbary Shore* and *The Deer Park*. Following the purgation and illumination represented by *Advertisements* they become, in the later novels *An American Dream* and *Why Are We in Vietnam?* and the related pieces in *The Presidential*

Papers and *Cannibals and Christians,* the consciously molded substance of Mailer's hypertrophic images of life in America at midcentury.

A detailed account of this course of change and growth must be left for later. The important fact is that after several more books, plus a string of other accomplishments — including play-producing, movie-making, a fling at architectural design, and a great deal of moral, social, and political punditing, both on paper and on the hoof — the author of *The Naked and the Dead* emerged in the mid-sixties, despite his still uncertain reputation among serious literary people, as decidedly the most active and vivid public figure on the American literary scene.

Like his first published novel and stories, Mailer's early life was at least conventional enough not to foreshadow with any definiteness the panoply of idiosyncrasy that was to come later. Born January 31, 1923, in Long Branch, New Jersey, to Isaac and Fanny Mailer, Norman Mailer was raised and schooled in Brooklyn, graduating from Boys High School in 1939. While at Harvard, where he earned a B.S. degree in aeronautical engineering in 1943, Mailer began writing in earnest, contributing to the *Advocate,* working at his first two (and still unpublished) novels, and winning in 1941 *Story* magazine's annual college fiction contest. In 1944 he married his first wife and was drafted into the army, serving in the Pacific Theater until 1946. During the next year and a half, part of which was spent in Europe, where he was enrolled as a student at the Sorbonne, Mailer wrote *The Naked and the Dead,* which was published with immediate and dramatic success. The public purchased it in such numbers that it held at the top of the best-seller lists for nearly three months. A movie contract was soon in the works; Lillian Hellman was slated to adapt it for the stage; and Sinclair Lewis was moved to dub Mailer "the greatest writer to come out of his generation."

8

Though Mailer himself once half-dismissed his first novel as a "conventional war novel," and though it was conceived and composed in a manner that Mailer was not to use again in a major work, *The Naked and the Dead* is much more than a "war novel." The embracing action of the novel — the taking of a Japanese-held Pacific island in World War II — is rendered with the skilled realist's commitment to the truthful and vivid depiction of actuality. But in the year of its publication Mailer put on record his view that *The Naked and the Dead*, though cast in the realist mold, is "symbolic," expressive of "death and man's creative urge, fate, man's desire to conquer the elements — all kinds of things you never dream of separating and stating so baldly." And there is no mistaking that the island itself, and the mountain at its center which Sergeant Croft commits himself and his platoon to conquering, acquire an almost Conradian symbolic significance in the eyes of their chief beholders. Here is the soldiers' vision of the setting of their destruction:

It was a sensual isle, a Biblical land of ruby wines and golden sands and indigo trees. The men stared and stared. The island hovered before them like an Oriental monarch's conception of heaven, and they responded to it with an acute and terrible longing. It was a vision of all the beauty for which they had ever yearned, all the ecstasy they had ever sought. For a few minutes it dissolved the long dreary passage of the mute months in the jungle, without hope, without pride. If they had been alone they might have stretched out their arms to it.

It could not last. Slowly, inevitably, the beach began to dissolve in the encompassing night. The golden sands grew faint, became gray-green, and darkened. The island sank into the water, and the tide of night washed over the rose and lavender hills. After a little while, there was only the gray-black ocean, the darkened sky, and the evil churning of the gray-white wake. Bits of phosphorescence swirled in the foam. The black dead ocean looked like a mirror of the night; it was cold, implicit with dread and death. The men felt it absorb them in a silent pervasive terror. They turned back

9

to their cots, settled down for the night, and shuddered for a long while in their blankets.

In an interview three years later, just after completing *Barbary Shore*, Mailer made this interesting disclosure about *The Naked and the Dead*: "I don't think of myself as a realist. That terrible word 'naturalism.' It was my literary heritage — the things I learned from Dos Passos and Farrell. I took naturally to it, that's the way one wrote a book. But I really was off on a mystic kick. Actually — a funny thing — the biggest influence on *Naked* was *Moby Dick*. . . . I was sure everyone would know. I had Ahab in it, and I suppose the mountain was Moby Dick. Of course, I also think the book will stand or fall as a realistic novel." This last qualification would also apply, of course, to *Moby Dick*. For Melville saw in the actual hazard and struggle of whaling, as Mailer did in war, the revealed pattern of the grandeur and tragedy of the whole human enterprise. Combat, for Mailer, is the chief means by which the higher laws of life become incarnate in human experience. War is his external subject matter in *The Naked and the Dead*; but his internal theme is the "crisis in human values" — identity, humanity, man, and the nature of their enemies in our time.

With war as the background typification of generalized external crisis, Mailer develops his internal themes by two principal means: first, extensively, through a number of Dos Passos-like diagnostic biographical portraits of a cross section of the fighting men; and second, intensively, through the protracted psychic struggle of mind and personality that takes place between Major General Cummings, the crypto-fascist commanding officer of the invading American forces, and his aide, a questioning liberal named Hearn. Both men have been shaped, though in opposite ways, by reaction against the privileged sterility of their midwestern bourgeois backgrounds. Cummings is the self-created prophet of a new totalitarianism who commands, in the name of his faith in order and authority, the breaking of men's spirits and the destruction of their wills. Hearn, bitter in his discontent, by nature a loner and yet tenderly humane in his half-guilty identification with the men he commands, is the uncertain voice of the liberal ideal of free man. Most of the fighting men are portrayed as already deprived, twisted, or stunted by the disintegrative and totalitarian forces and counterforces at work in their world, the forces whose contention has culminated in the war which now envelops them all. These men are the data of the dialectical contest which is taking place between Cummings and Hearn. That contest, the original of similar recurring patterns of individual contest, including sexual, in most of the rest of Mailer's work, ends in a kind of draw. Hearn and his convictions are wasted when he dies as a casual accident of war on an irrelevant mission. And though the campaign is won, Cummings is in essence defeated because the agency of victory is not his active military intelligence but rather a chain of chance accidents beyond his control.

One notices not only that a true hero is lacking from the novel's epic-like action, but that his opposite, a forceful antagonist, is lacking too. And yet a large enveloping energy has gathered, thrust forward, and come through to significant issue. A great spasm of nature, an inevitable motion of history, has superseded the efficacies of individual men in a world that has begun to move across Yeats's threshold of apocalypse where "the best lack all conviction" and "the worst/are full of passionate intensity."

But at the core of this vast action, his presence stressing the hero's absence, is Sergeant Croft. After the death of Hearn, he leads the platoon on its doomed assault upon the mountain, dominating his men by the sheer intensity of his undefined "hunger" for the mastery of life. A rough prototype of D. J. Jethroe of *Why Are We in Vietnam?*, Croft has been sired by a tough Texas dirt-farmer

on a woman conventionally "weak . . . sweet and mild." His
father encourages in him a predator's taste for hunting, and he is
by nature "mean." Why? "Oh, there are answers. He is that way
because of the corruption-of-the-society. He is that way because
the devil has claimed him for one of his own. It is because he is
a Texan; it is because he has renounced God." The author inter-
prets Croft in an aside as follows: *He hated weakness and he loved
practically nothing. There was a crude unformed vision in his
soul but he was rarely conscious of it.*" This embryonic "vision"
is different from Hearn's superannuated liberalism and Cummings'
authoritarian calculus because it is an animal thing — an energy
with fierce tendencies but no "form." Croft represents the kinetic
life-substance upon which such alternative ideologies as those of
Hearn and Cummings must depend for their unforeseeable realizations. In his irrational will and passion, he is the human microcosm of the vast upsurge of inhuman forces in history which express themselves in the ironic irresolutions of the total action of
The Naked and the Dead.

The Naked and the Dead, then, even if substantially conventional in form and style, is nevertheless one with the rest of Mailer's
work in the apocalyptic energies of its vision. Those energies begin
to find their requisite new form, and with that a new sort of voice,
in the first of Mailer's "experimental" novels, *Barbary Shore,* published in 1951. *Barbary Shore* was the product, as Mailer has written
in retrospect, "of intense political preoccupation and a voyage in
political affairs which began with the Progressive Party and has
ended in the *cul-de-sac* (at least so far as action is concerned) of
being an anti-Stalinist Marxist who feels that war is probably inevitable." The omniscient authorial point of view of *The Naked
and the Dead* is abandoned in *Barbary Shore* for first-person narrative, which is to continue as the preferred narrative form for
Mailer's books thereafter. ("Memory is the seed of narrative, yeah,"

says D. J. Jethroe, narrator of *Why Are We in Vietnam?*) The book becomes, thus, an adaptation of *Bildungsroman*; its narrative substance is the hero's education for life in our time — or re-education, since he is suffering from amnesia somewhat inexplicitly induced by war and the breakdown of traditional political idealism. The setting is a Brooklyn rooming house operated by a sexually promiscuous and morally neuter proprietress named, with an irony appropriate to her role as life's presiding norm, Guinevere. In this setting, the case histories of three roomers are presented: an impotent, betrayed, and self-betraying idealist of the old revolutionary left; his demon, a stolid and perverted interrogator for the rightist "totalitarian" establishment; and a mad Cassandra-like girl whose derangement is a consequence and expression of history, and whom, as an exacerbated mirroring of his own distressed psyche, the hero half loves.

The heaviness and inertia of the novel — its garrulous expositions of ideological conflict and the dazed passivity and blankness of Lovett, the hero-narrator, before all he sees and hears — is only a little relieved when at the end he sprints into an inchoate future with a mysterious small object entrusted to his keeping by the failed leftist before his death. The precise nature of the object, which is hotly coveted by the furies of the right, is never specified. But what it means is perfectly clear. It is a symbol or talisman of the sacred idea of man free and whole; and in the moment of the narrator's active commitment to it in the face of the terrible odds and enemies ranged against it, and now against him as well, we are meant to feel that it has taken on the existential power of life itself.

Even this early in his career — after only two novels — it is clear that Mailer's imagination, unique in his generation, is cast in the epic mold. As bard and prophet to an age in which history is at odds with nature or "destiny," he tells in a fevered voice of the permutations of the heroic imperative in a post-heroic world. His theme is the struggle of life and form against death and chaos. But his subject matter is history. And as he pursues the theme of the ideal through the matter of the actual he makes a discovery: in our time the sources and resources of life have shifted, to use the shorthand of Mailer's own symbology, from "God" to "the devil." The vision of life at stalemate in *The Naked and the Dead* and *Barbary Shore* is explained by this discovery, a discovery whose fullness of realization in a changed imaginative vision comes clear in *The Deer Park*, published in 1955.

Desert D'Or, a resort of the rich and powerful modeled on Palm Springs, is the principal setting of *The Deer Park*. It is a denatured interior world of concrete and plastic, of harsh light and blinding shadow, thrown up in defiance of the encircling desert outside. This pattern of division between natural and unnatural that is established in the setting extends also to the characters, in whom desire and will, feeling and thought, the wellsprings of motive and motive's fulfillment in action, have been stricken apart. The natural current of the life-force has somehow been broken. And the inhabitants of this world of trauma and aftermath constitute a gallery of parodies of the human image ranging from the absurd to the piteous to the monstrous. They are, as Mailer wrote in a note to his adaptation of *The Deer Park* for the stage, "in hell."

Sergius O'Shaugnessy, the hero-narrator of *The Deer Park*, is both an orphan and, like Lovett of *Barbary Shore*, a symbolic waif of historical disaster. His surrogate home in the air force and fulfillment in the exercise of the war pilot's impersonal skills of destruction have been snatched from him in a sudden accidental revelation that he is a killer: "I realized that . . . I had been busy setting fire to a dozen people, or two dozen, or had it been a hundred?" In recoil from such horrors of the "real world" he suffers a breakdown, is discharged, and on the winnings from a prodigiously lucky gambling venture, he comes to Desert D'Or, retreat of the gods of the "imaginary world," to rest, drift, gaze, and spend. A blank slate to be written on, an empty vessel to be filled, and — his vision of the burned flesh of his victims having rendered him sexually impotent — a low flame needing fuel, Sergius O'Shaugnessy is the framing consciousness of an ample world crowded with people exhibiting versions of his own predicament. Among the most important of these are Charles Francis Eitel, a gifted and formerly powerful Hollywood director, and Marion Faye, dope pusher, impresario of call girls, and connoisseur of the moral nuances of sadism. Both of these men become friends of O'Shaugnessy and objects of his studious moral attention.

Eitel has had a golden age, a brief heroic period in the thirties when as a true artist he made courageous movies on contemporary social themes, and when as a man of integrity he put his life on the line in behalf of the fated struggle for democracy in Spain. In reflexive response to the corruption of integrity which has overtaken his art as he has risen to power in Hollywood, Eitel rebuffs a congressional investigating committee seeking from him incriminating political testimony against his colleagues. In consequence, the industry blackballs him; and his loss of power and identity in the "imaginary" world is measured in personal terms by his loss of potency as both artist and lover. This sequential pattern of aspiration, action, corruption, moral illumination, renunciation, exile, and impotence precisely parallels the pattern of Sergius' life. Eitel is the distillate of the best values of the past by which Sergius has been fathered and orphaned, and for Sergius, consequently, the question of Eitel's destiny — the question of his potential for rebirth and self-renewal — has crucial moral significance.

Eitel stumbles upon a "second chance" in the form of Elena Esposito, and he muffs it. Another man's castoff, she is soiled, tawdry, and simple. She is a poor dancer and a worse actress, and her manners are absurd. And yet she has the dignity and courage, and finally the beauty, of a being wholly natural. Eitel's affair with her becomes the nourishing ground of a new life for him. His sexual potency is restored, and with it his creative potency as he begins to work on a script which he imagines will be the redemption of his integrity as artist and man. But this new access of life fills him with fear; it is the stirring in him of the heroic imperative, with its attendant commitments to solitary battle, lonely journeyings in the unknown, and the risks of failure and defeat. The doors of Hollywood begin to open again, and the thrones and dominations of the "imaginary" world solicit his return: all he must do is confess and recant before the committee, and he may pass back through those doors. Half because of fear, half because of old habit, Eitel takes the easy way of surrender, shunning the hazardous alternatives (as Elena, significantly, does not) represented by those dark angels of life and truth, Don Beda, high priest of satyrism and orgy, and Marion Faye, the hipster prophet of criminal idealism. His harvest is the life-in-death of security through compromise, the corruption of his script and his talent, and eventual marriage to a broken and exhausted Elena, which is possible now that they are no longer "wedded" in a sacramental sense.

Elena is a noble figure — defeated, but honorably so, in her fated but heroic contest with time and what Hardy calls "crass casualty." Eitel's enemies have been lesser ones — history and social circumstance — and his defeat is pitiful rather than noble, because he has "sold out." But he has at least the saving grace of his ironic intelligence, which enables him to understand, when she proudly refuses his first offer of marriage, the principle of Elena's nobility: "the essence of spirit . . . was to choose the thing which did not better one's position but made it more perilous." Later on, when she has no more resources of refusal and he nourishes upon her defeat by "sacrificing" himself in marrying her, he under-

stands his own corresponding cowardice: "there was that law of life so cruel and so just which demanded that one must grow or else pay more for remaining the same."
Eitel is Mailer's version of the traditional hero in his last historical incarnation. Vision, passion, and courage have dwindled in Eitel to intelligence, compassion, and guilt — the "cement" of the world, as Marion Faye contemptuously labels the last two, which binds men, enfeebles them, and turns them into spiritual "slobs." Eitel's very strengths are weaknesses, his virtues are faults, in a world where the apocalyptic beasts of anxiety and dread are raging in prisons of compromise and falsehood. And as the novel draws to its close and Eitel begins to fade into the penumbra of Sergius O'Shaugnessy's memorializing imagination, we are aware that the passing of the man is also the passing of the values he represented. Flanked by comic Lulu Meyers, a movie sex goddess who on impulse marries for "love" rather than career, and by tragic Marion Faye whose anarch's code of black moral reason leads him behind prison bars, the now enlightened Sergius is the chief chalice-bearer of new human values. He becomes a bullfighter, stud, and teacher of both arts. And he begins to write, his books presumably fired by the existential perils and ecstasies of combat and sexuality. Though the novel ends on a cheerful note of metaphysical exhilaration, Sergius, both as a character and as an archetype of new styles of human value, is vague and inchoate as well as faintly absurd. Sergius has survived all sorts of traumas and temptations and come through to freedom, but he is not very much more fully realized as an examplar of new values in action than was his predecessor, Lovett. He has come to terms with the world that has wounded him, and like the good Emersonian "fatalists" that all such Mailer heroes are, he affirms it as his destined inheritance from nature and history. But neither he nor his author has yet found the requisite life-style, the new heroic mold through which

to turn understanding and affirmation into creative, perhaps re-demptive action.

Life threatened in our time by the forces of death is Mailer's subject everywhere. When he writes as a realist, as in *The Naked and the Dead*, life is stalemated and defeated by the forces of death. In the next two novels the intensities of anxiety and dread un-derlying Mailer's subject matter begin to dominate the rational, circumjacent forms of the realist, distorting them in the direction of the expressionistic and the surreal. And with this modification of form comes a coordinate modification of the heroes in whom the issue of the life-death struggle is finally centered. The narrator-hero of *Barbary Shore*, for whom the action encompassed by his consciousness is an elaborately instructive morality play, in the end escapes paralysis and spiritual death. The similarly educated narrator-hero of *The Deer Park* not only escapes but, as he bids fond farewell to the memories of the defeated and destroyed, dis-cerns in the very chemistry of the disease and decomposition all around him the flicker and spur of new possibilities for life. "Think of Sex as Time," says "God" in a final dialogue with Sergius, "and Time as the connection of new circuits."

Barbary Shore and *The Deer Park*, both of them fictional in-vestigations of the operative laws of death and endings, are novels that end with beginnings. Mailer's next novel, *An American Dream*, published in 1965, is in every way an extension and in-tensification of the manner and substance of its two predecessors. It begins, significantly, with an ending: the hero saves himself from spiritual death by committing a murder that restores him to life, action, growth. Seen in relation to *An American Dream*, the two preceding novels have the look of a single imaginative action of a precursory nature: a complex psycho-dramatic "sloughing-off," to use Lawrence's terms in *Studies in Classic American Literature*, of the "old consciousness" of an outworn idealistic humanism in preparation for a "new consciousness" requisite for survival and significant life in a psychotic world bordering on apocalypse and yearning toward death. The experiential educations of Mikey Lovett and Sergius O'Shaugnessy in *Barbary Shore* and *The Deer Park* are preparations of this "new consciousness" for active engagement with the world. Steve Rojack and D. J. Jethroe — respectively heroes of *An American Dream* and *Why Are We in Vietnam?* — are the beneficiaries of this process. Rojack, in a moment of freeing impulse, murders his rich, preternaturally domineering, death-threatening wife Deborah, a "bitch-goddess" of American power, and the summation of the death-force of historical fate. The charge of this self-galvanizing destruction of his immediate enemy propels him into action, turning fear, fatigue, and despair into a redemptive energy of desperation. With a courage nourished on the ultimate dread, the dread of death, he runs a varied course of triumphs — besting the sexual enmity of a cold nymphomaniac, the hunting wile of the police, the competition of a Negro stud of legendary sexual prowess, and an engulfing sea of guilt and self-doubt summoned by Deborah's father, Barney Kelly. He even finds love along the way, with a tender, used, and charming cabaret singer named Cherry. A composite of American realities like Deborah, she is Deborah's opposite and complement, a plucky victim of the forces of which Deborah is the emblematic goddess and proprietress. At the end Rojack is still running — his roles and costumes of war hero, congressman, professor, television personality, and husband of a socialite left far behind — now toward the darker and simpler challenges of the jungles of Guatemala and Yucatán.

In *Why Are We in Vietnam?* (1967), D. J. Jethroe has already reached his Guatemala and Yucatán. High on pot, the prose of the Marquis de Sade and William Burroughs, and the cheerfully psychotic inspiration that he may be the voice of a "Harlem spade" imprisoned in the body of the son of a white Dallas tycoon, he tells the story of how he got that way. It is an initiation story (new style) as *An American Dream* was a new-style story of sacrifice and redemption. The initiation, product of a hunting "safari" to Alaska with his father Rusty, D. J.'s best friend Tex, and assorted guides and associates, has two phases, both of them involving radical divestments and ultimate tests of courage. In the first phase, D. J. breaks spiritually with his father when, out of habits of competitive vanity and self-justification, his father claims the grizzly bear that D. J. has mortally wounded, violating not only the father-son bond as reinforced by the hunt (stalking their dangerous quarry D. J. sees himself and his father as "war buddies") but also the sacred blood bond between killer and prey. Thinks D. J., "Final end of love of one son for one father." The second phase of the initiation, fruit of the alienation and frustration sown by the first, is the twenty-four-hour northward foray of D. J. and Tex, alone and without guns or instruments, into the wild heart of the Brooks Range. In an ecstasy of fear and trembling they witness a pageant of savageries — wolf, eagle, bear, caribou, and moose, the figments of natural life locked in struggle with death — culminating in a cosmic eruption of the Northern Lights that is so magnificent and intense as to bring them to the border of orgy and fratricide: "they were twins, never to be as lovers again, but killer brothers, armed by something, prince of darkness, lord of light, they did not know." They make a bond in an exchange of blood, "the deep beast whispering, Fulfill my will, go forth and kill." At the end, D. J., now eighteen, looks beyond the Brooks Range of his initiatory "Guatemala and Yucatán" toward his mature destiny: "Hot damn, Vietnam."

D. J. is the voice of the anxieties and compulsions that have accumulated beneath the patterns of America's history and exploded at last in the manifest violence and chaos of its present. In the electric North, which is the voltaic pile of a continent's repressed, distorted, and perverted life-energies, he has faced Demo-gorgon, and he comes back metamorphosed, a rudely American voice of bardic ecstasy and prophecy. Completing the journey of transformation only begun by Lovett and Sergius O'Shaugnessy, D. J. and Steve Rojack have successfully tracked the power of life, thieved by a conspiracy of history with nature from its traditional home in the light, to its new home in darkness. In accomplishing this, they become exemplars of that "new consciousness" requisite to continuing life's ancient battle against death in a psychotic world bordering on apocalyptic crisis.

Richard Poirier, identifying Mailer with Eliot's vision, sees him as similarly spurred by the "de-creative" aspects of creation. But if this is true, Mailer is even more closely related to Lawrence, who in the voice of Rupert Birkin of *Women in Love* discerned among the "marsh-flowers" of "destructive creation" certain blossoms that while they were spawned by the all-enveloping historical process of "universal dissolution" were not *"fleurs du mal,"* but rather "roses, warm and flamy." Lawrence himself was one of these exotic exceptions. And so is Mailer. If the roots of both writers necessarily nourish upon the food of darkness, the blossoms produced are bright with the warm colors of life, and grow toward the light. In Lawrence the blossom is the "man who has come through," the separate natural self released through the death of the conventional social self into a living and changing "star-equilibrium" with the otherness of nature and woman. In Mailer it is all this and a bit more: history, impelled by the American dream turned to nightmare, is a third constituent of the otherness, and the reborn self becomes an "existential hero."

Advertisements for Myself (1959) and *The Presidential Papers* (1963) are large and various but nevertheless unified collections of pieces, mostly nonfiction, written during the dozen years following Mailer's tentative effort and partial failure to achieve a new form in *Barbary Shore*. As books principally about their author, *Advertisements for Myself* and *The Presidential Papers* taken together have the shape, like *Barbary Shore* and *The Deer Park*, of a single action, the complex and difficult action of "sloughing off" the "old consciousness." "The existential hero," first coming to full life in *An American Dream* and *Why Are We in Vietnam?*, is Mailer's realization of this new style of consciousness. And *Advertisements for Myself* and *The Presidential Papers* are the record of its gestation in the mind of its creator, and of the large and small deaths prerequisite to its coming to birth.

Mailer uses his own "personality," he tells us, as the "armature" of *Advertisements* — an image aptly descriptive of both its form and its impact. The reciprocal emotions of dread and determination whirl at the center of the book, as its author frankly appraises, at mid-career, his qualified victories and larger defeats during more than a decade of trying to live up to his potentials and ambitions as a man and writer. The pieces collected in *Advertisements* — stories, essays, and poems; polemics, meditations, and interviews; fragments of plays-in-progress and novels-to-be — are the measure of the worth of the life being lived, the substance of the tale being told. It is a tale, like Fitzgerald's in "The Crack-Up" essays, of early success, subsequent failure and demoralization, and the reflexive counterthrust of self-regeneration and re-creation. *The Naked and the Dead*, which catapulted him to sudden and youthful fame, had, as he tells us in *Advertisements*, been "easy to write." But nothing would be so easy again, for this success was the beginning of his "existentialism," which was "forced upon [him]," as he says, by his finding himself "prominent and empty," a "personage," at twenty-five. He must justify the prominence and fill the emptiness. With such heroic models before him as the lifestyle of Hemingway and the *oeuvre* of Malraux, he thrusts experimentally into new territory with *Barbary Shore*, "the first of the existentialist novels in America." The hostility and ridicule with which it is greeted in 1951 knock him down. Deflated, ill, and anxious, he turns to writing "respectable" short stories in the earlier manner and jaunty socio-political polemics for such magazines as *Partisan Review* and *Dissent* (of which he also becomes an editor). All this is a sort of distraction and temporizing in the face of the big comeback, the planned colossal counterpunch which might dazzle the world with a starfall and revelations: a projected eight-volume novel of cosmic proportions whose framing consciousness, a minor man and an artist *manqué* named Sam Slovoda, has an alter ego dream-hero named Sergius O'Shaugnessy. The great work hovering in the wings refuses to emerge. But two related fragments appear, both of them again in the new manner: the story "The Man Who Loved Yoga," which is to be the great work's prologue, and a protracted but relevant detour from the main route, a novel called *The Deer Park*.

The story of the vicissitudes accompanying *The Deer Park*'s publication and reception, most of it recounted in *Advertisements*, could itself be the stuff of a novel. The bad reception of *Barbary Shore* in 1951 and Mailer's divorce in 1952 are elements of a continuing pattern of gathering personal distress which characterize the years of *The Deer Park*'s composition. These distresses reach a penultimate crisis when *The Deer Park*, already in page proof, is suddenly held up by its publisher: Stanley Rinehart finds in it something unacceptably obscene. Just recently Mailer has accepted the challenge of writing an essay called "The Homosexual Villain" at the invitation of the magazine *One*, an undertaking which has blown up a "log jam of accumulated timidities and restraints" in him. Partially as a consequence, he refuses to make the change in *The Deer Park* for Rinehart, and the deal is off. The next ten weeks, at the end of which *The Deer Park* will be accepted by Putnam after refusal by several other houses, is a time of crisis for Mailer. He has undergone another death — the death of certain illusions about himself as "a figure in the landscape," and about the "honor" of publishers and writers in the American present — and feels himself becoming a "psychic outlaw."

Drawing his powers now from forays into the worlds of jazz, Harlem, and marijuana, he sees that the style of *The Deer Park* is wrong for the narrator he wants to create — it is too poetic, in the vein of Fitzgerald's Nick Carraway. He begins to rewrite from page proof, thirsting for the kind of self-redemptive success which would change the world a little, and at the same time dreading the possibility of a bad reception and low sales. The revised *The Deer Park*, once published, is only a "middling success." And Mailer measures the quality of its success not only by sales and reviews but by the glimpses of possibility that have begun to emerge for the harried author with his last-minute impetus to rewrite it. Though tentative and incomplete, the accomplished changes adumbrate a new hero: the tender, wounded, and detached observer of the earlier version has begun to turn into a Sergius O'Shaugnessy who is not only "good" but also "ambitious"; a Sergius who, instead of virtuously spurning Hollywood's offer to film his life, might have taken the bait in a spirit of adventure and run it to some perilous triumph. The published book, its author laments, is but a hint of what might have been: the masterpiece in Mailer's generation equivalent to *The Sun Also Rises* in Hemingway's. As a "middling success," *The Deer Park* represents to its author his gross failure to bid on "the biggest hand" he had ever held, and a discovery that after all he hadn't the magic to "hasten the time of apocalypse."

But even so, this fumble, this failure, is no dead end. Like the emptiness of his success with *The Naked and the Dead*, and the fullness of his failure with *Barbary Shore*, it is a threshold to possibility. He has a vision, now, of what he must try to be and do as a writer, and of how considerable are the odds ranged against him. And like Sergius, who takes up bullfighting at the end of *The Deer Park*, he moves directly into the arena of the world's action as a matador of existential polemics — a rebel general of "Hip" — in the pages of *The Village Voice*, which he helped found in 1955. Though a fresh excursion into novel-writing is delayed by these side trips into journalism, *The Village Voice* pieces are important as snapshots of the "new" Mailer soon fully to emerge as exemplar and spokesman of the needed "new consciousness." His first important effort in the new mode is the essay *The White Negro*, written in 1957 and first published, by City Lights, in 1958 (it was reprinted in *Advertisements*).

A speculative psycho-cultural essay on the modern predicament, *The White Negro* is a paradigm of the vision, the ideas, the motifs and symbols that will shape all of Mailer's future work in whatever form. The Hipster refuses to capitulate to the repressive denaturing, dehumanizing death-force of a "totalitarian" society. But because he is active — unlike the bourgeois "beat" who withdraws and passively sublimates in the surrogate quasi-life of song, flowers, meditation, hallucinogens, and "love" — he is confronted by the immediate dangers of physical violence and death. Like the Negro he is an *un*citizen (hence the label "white Negro") and danger is the medium of his life. Pleasure is his end; energy, courage, and wile are his means. The dynamic poise of his life-style implies the constitution, in microcosm, of a whole culture: decorums of manners, dress, language; an ethic; an aesthetic; even, finally, a metaphysic and a theology. The philosophy of the Hip, Mailer reflects, is the formed insight of a "radical humanist" "brooding" on the energizing phenomenon of the Negro revolution in contemporary America.

The Hipster is, of course, only one of many possible realizations of the "new consciousness" of which Mailer is the prophet. He is but one version of the idea of the existential hero, whose incarnation not only *may* but *must* be limitless and unpredictable. For the existential hero is the Dostoevskian underground man come aboveground into the Tolstoian mainstream of history. It is not known what he will be there, only that he will *do* — his being a function of his acting, rather than the other way around. He is a Sisyphus released from the stone of his dogged abstract commitment, a Hemingway galvanized into new life by the very terrors that threaten paralysis and death. Evading the fateful impasse between heroic "intactness" and human "completeness" that destroyed Fitzgerald's Dick Diver, he is a vital synthesis of the polar values of self-control and spontaneity represented in *The Deer Park* by Marion Faye, the black puritan of moral scruple, and Don Beda, the rosy orgiast of the senses. Extensively educated in anguish, division, and impotence, Sergius O'Shaugnessy has just touched the regenerative power of that synthesis when the book of his salvation closes. The same efflorescence in his creator, which achieves full bloom in *The Presidential Papers*, seems to have been nourished by a similar curriculum, as recounted in *Advertisements*, of prior defeats and despairs. *Advertisements*, in contrast to its successor, *The Presidential Papers*, is a book in the mode of elegy, recording in lyric regret and anger the difficult passing of romantic idealism and the death of youth's illusions. But *Advertisements* also has elegy's *dramatic* mode, being shaped as a total action embodying patterns of divestment and purgation which yield up at last a clear prospect of fresh possibilities: "Tomorrow to fresh woods, and pastures new." *The White Negro*, which Mailer tells us was written in the depths of "fear that I was no longer a writer," turns out to be the bright and central song of a "man who has come through." It is after all, he sees, one of his "best things." In it, and in the two late stories in the "existential" mode, "The Time of Her

Time" and "Advertisements for Myself on the Way Out," published at the close of *Advertisements*, can be found, as he says, "the real end of this muted autobiography of the near-beat adventurer who was myself."

The end of a life, whether well or badly lived, Mailer writes in *Advertisements*, is "seed." The "seed" of the agonies survived by the hero of *Advertisements* is *The Presidential Papers*, in which the author steps forth, re-created as public man and existentialist prophet, to address America and its leaders on the exigent realities of the age.

The "armature" of this book is not the author's personality in crisis, but rather an *idea* — the idea of "existential politics": "Existential politics is simple. It has a basic argument: if there is a strong ineradicable strain in human nature, one must not try to suppress it or anomaly, cancer and plague will follow. Instead one must find an art into which it can grow." In *The Presidential Papers* the pattern of personal crisis and salvation of self traced in *Advertisements* has been transmuted, by the chemistry of analogy so characteristic of Mailer's imagination, into the public terms of politics and history. But though the drama is now public rather than private, Mailer's self is no less central to the action. In the preface to *The Presidential Papers* he defines his role: to infuse John F. Kennedy, whose glamour and magnetism give him the potential of an "existential hero" in the arena of politics, with the requisite "existential" political consciousness. Mailer's commitment here is to steal back, for the languishing forces of "God," some of the energies of life which have passed over to the forces of darkness. But because history has moved so far on the downward path of de-creation, he must do it as a kind of undercover agent: he must perforce speak as a "devil." His first success as a metaphysical Robin Hood is his brilliant *Esquire* piece on Kennedy's nomination by the 1960 Democratic convention, which was written, despite his candidate's moribund "liberal" program, for the purpose of getting this rare man, so blessed "with a face," elected. For it is Mailer's belief that this essay, a product of his "Faustian" pact with "Mephisto," was the generative cause of Kennedy's small plurality over Nixon in the election. The rest of *The Presidential Papers* is a contemporaneous critique (with the blood, sweat, and tears of immediate response staining the pages) of "the Kennedy years," that ambiguous and perhaps despair-making hisorical return on its author's original existential wager.

Of all the fine pieces following, perhaps the most memorable is the essay on the Patterson-Liston fight, subtitled "Death." This essay is many things: It is a skillful piece of evocative journalism about an actual event; a symbolist's reading of the forces at war in the submerged psyche of America; a strange, oblique prophesy, through a poet's analysis of the attrition and inevitable doom of the spirit of American liberal idealism, of Kennedy's assassination. It is also a gaily profound exploration of the absurdity, and perhaps the peril, awaiting the writer as performing tragic-comedian whose ambition is to ride at the same time both bright Pegasus and the dark horses of wrath. But if the end — or "seed" — of life is life itself, then that effort must be made in spite of all hazard: "To believe the impossible may be won," Mailer writes elsewhere in *The Presidential Papers*, "creates a strength from which the impossible may be attacked." And in our time, though the memory of "God" and the light may shape ultimate heroic purpose, the hero draws nourishment for his "humanism" (a favorite recurring word of Mailer's) from the devil's realm, venturing ever more deeply — as Mailer does in the barbarous poems and scatological dialogues collected in *Cannibals and Christians* — into the territories of darkness.

Cannibals and Christians, published in 1966, is not so good a book as its two omnibus predecessors, though it has its bright spots,

such as the piece on Goldwater's nomination and the temptation
it wakens in its author to ride this newest bandwagon of the devil.
The drama of self-discovery and re-creation, which gave unity to
the brilliance and variety of *Advertisements* and *Papers*, is slowed
and muffled in *Cannibals* by the didactic accents of the guru who
gazes upon a vision that is cooling toward dogma and repetition.
But it is perhaps understandable that the imaginative break-
through represented by *An American Dream* should be followed
by a somewhat studious contemplation of the truths revealed, for
something more than half of the stuff of *Cannibals* was written
shortly after *Dream*. Mailer himself seems to be aware of the condition. Written in a time of "plague" and under a lurid cloud of
apocalyptic expectations, the collection is concerned with themes,
he says, more appropriate to a novel. He feels again the impulse
to "go back to that long novel, announced six years ago, and
changed in the mind by all of seven years." *Cannibals*, he reflects,
may be the last such collection for a while.

Since *Cannibals*, in addition to publishing *Why Are We in
Vietnam?* Mailer has produced off Broadway his dramatization of
The Deer Park, a crisply successful play in which a much clearer
and more effective Sergius O'Shaugnessy has been purchased at the
expense of the novel's richly internal realization of Eitel and Elena.
He has also directed, produced, and starred in two full-length
"existential" films of his own conceiving. The requisite honors
have begun, belatedly, to come his way: in 1967 he was elected to
the National Institute of Arts and Letters. And in October of the
same year, this author of twelve books, father of six children, and
veteran of four wives — "heroines all," he has gallantly affirmed —
proved his continued interest in the public life of his time by
getting himself arrested, jailed, and fined for an act of civil dis-
obedience in the great Washington demonstrations against the war
in Vietnam.

The immediate result of this was *The Armies of the Night*, published in the spring of 1968, a kind of autobiographical novel with a protagonist called "Mailer" who is at once an absurd citizen of "technology-land" in crisis and a bard of the bright dream that lies behind the thickening miasmas of the betrayed and perishing republic. It is unquestionably one of Mailer's best books — passionate, humorous, acutely intelligent, and, as always, eloquent in its empathy with the drift of history. It has new riches in it, too, of a more incidental kind, such as a gallery of sharply intimate verbal cartoons, highlighted with the reflected pigments of Mailer's own uniquely anxious self-image, of such primary men of our moment as Robert Lowell, Dwight Macdonald, and Paul Goodman. But most striking of all are its undercurrents of a softer emotion than we have been used to finding in Mailer, a new tenderness for life that lets him muse warmly along the way on his troubled love for his wife, his children, his mythic America. There is even a touch of nostalgic religious craving in it, a small recurring thirst for "Christ." But though the texture of feeling is more varied, the old Mailer, familiarly gravid with the epic furies and ambitions of a diminutive Brooklyn Achilles, still prevails:

Mailer, looking back, thought bitter words he would not say: "You, Lowell, beloved poet of many, what do you know of the dirt and the dark deliveries of the necessary? What do you know of dignity hard-achieved, and dignity lost through innocence, and dignity lost by sacrifice for a cause one cannot name? What do you know about getting fat against your will, and turning into a clown of an arriviste baron when you would rather be an eagle or a count, or rarest of all, some natural aristocrat from these damned democratic states? No, the only subject we share, you and I, is that species of perception which shows that if we are not very loyal to our unendurable and most exigent inner light, then some day we may burn. How dare you condemn me! . . . How dare you scorn the explosive I employ?"

Lowell falls backward at this moment in the narrative, a noble Hector going bump on his head, as if toppled by the lightning bolt of his adversary's thought. Though *The Armies of the Night* is tempered with new softnesses and warmths, such passages would deter one from concluding too easily that Mailer may be getting ready to write his hymn of reconciliation — his *Tempest* or "Lapis Lazuli," his *Billy Budd* or *Old Man and the Sea.*

Good as *The Armies of the Night* is, and prolific in a variety of media as Mailer has been in the last decade, the great opus so long ago announced remains unachieved. Are such varied and frequent detours from the high road of novel-writing threatening, at this prime of his creative life, the ultimate dissipation of Mailer's talent as a major writer? This already familiar question was raised yet again by an interviewer in *Playboy* for January 1968. Mailer answered that the pattern of his career was dictated by his instinctive feeling that "the best way to grow was not to write one novel after another but to move from activity to activity, a notion that began with Renaissance man." He does not mention the example of Milton, but he might as well have. Then, coming down off the high horse of the moment's rhetoric, he adds genially, "It's not my idea, after all."

He is, of course, right both about himself and about "the tradition." With the romantic movement the imaginative writer became alienated from public life. Next, under the neoclassical reactive pressure of modernist formalism, he became in a sense alienated even from his work — which was not to be an utterance but an object, a product of the "impersonal" operations of imagination. With this background in view, it is clear that Mailer's uniqueness as a mid-century writer lies in his conscious cultivation, in the manner of Yeats, of a dynamic interrelation between his art and his life-style. Intensely himself, he is nevertheless the writer reborn in the dimension of public man. Engorged with the inclusive themes of his age and his nation, his work is nevertheless deeply personal. "I've been working on one book most of my life," he told the *Playboy* interviewer. "Probably since I started with *Barbary Shore*, certainly with and since *The Deer Park*, I've been working on one book." As he tells us in the introduction to *Cannibals and Christians*, he is, like Lawrence, Henry Miller, and Hemingway, writing "one continuing book . . . of [his] life and the vision of [his] existence." He might also have mentioned Fitzgerald whom he resembles in this respect as well as in many others, including his sense of the integral relation between the moral health of the artist and the quality of his art conceived as "style." "A really good style," said Mailer in his *Paris Review* interview of 1964, as if in echo of a dozen similar testimonies by Fitzgerald, "comes only when a man has become as good as he can be. Style is character."

"Style," broadly understood as the individual humane stance a writer chooses to take in relation to his material along its whole spectrum from language to vision, is perhaps the judgmental critic's most useful tool in approaching such a writer. For both the strengths and weaknesses of Mailer's work are the products of his unique commitment to being as "good," and thus as creative, a man as he can.

As recently as the early sixties, fairly literate people — often critics and teachers — were still saying that though Mailer certainly had a novelist's gift he "couldn't write." He was in their minds a kind of James Jones who, with no appropriate arsenal of sophistication, had gone adventuring into frontier territories of the imagination and was never heard of again. "I can't read him any more," they would say; and it was at least evident that these people who made themselves responsible for keeping up with Bellow and Malamud, Styron and Barth — current writers favored with recognition by the critical establishment — *weren't* reading him, whether or not they *couldn't* read him. To them he was at once nuttier than D. H. Lawrence, dumber than Sinclair Lewis, artistically more unselective even than Thomas Wolfe, these faults clumsily wrapped in a style a good deal more wooden and awkward than Dreiser's. Because they weren't reading him it wasn't possible to argue with any hope of success that his "beliefs" were the poetical vehicles of a metaphysician's speculative insights; that he was the only important novelist on the American scene who was also an authentic and sophisticated intellectual; that if he was temperamentally the inclusive artist, he was also deftly capable of the lean and compact virtuoso performance; and that his style — ranging the spectrum from slang to sublimity — was a distillate of all the rest into a shimmering and variegated brilliancy of words. An example from *The Armies of the Night*:

There was an aesthetic economy to symbolic gestures — you must not repeat yourself. Arrested once, TV land would accept him (conceivably) as a man willing to stand up for his ideas; get busted twice on the same day, and they would view him as a freak-out panting for arrest. (Mailer's habit of living — no matter how unsuccessfully — with his image, was so ingrained by now, that like a dutiful spouse he was forever consulting his better half.)

This is the style incisive, the author cutting an idea down to the gem of epigram at its center. An example from *The Presidential Papers*:

It is the wisdom of a man who senses death within him and gambles that he can cure it by risking his life. It is the therapy of the instinct, and who is so wise as to call it irrational? Before he went into the Navy, Kennedy had been ailing. Washed out of Freshman year at Princeton by a prolonged trough of yellow jaundice, sick for a year at Harvard, weak already in the back from an injury at football, his trials suggest the self-hatred of a man whose resentment and ambition are too large for his body. Not everyone can discharge their furies on an analyst's couch, for some angers can be relaxed only by winning power, some rages are sufficiently monu-

mental to demand that one try to become a hero or else fall back
into that death which is already within the cells. But if one suc-
ceeds, the energy aroused can be exceptional. . . . One thinks
of that three-mile swim with the belt in his mouth and McMahon
holding it behind him. There are pestilences which sit in the mouth
and rot the teeth — in those five hours how much of the psyche
must have been remade, for to give vent to the bite in one's jaws
and yet use that rage to save a life: it is not so very many men who
have the apocalyptic sense that heroism is the First Doctor. . . .
With such a man in office the myth of the nation would again be
engaged . . .

This is the style progenitive, the author pushing out from the central root-and-trunk idea a branch-bud-and-leaf exfoliation of con-
firmatory images.

Mailer's style is a style of eddying gusts and pointed audible si-
lences textured on a background of the musing, ruminating, won-
dering human voice. Voice is the style's medium; its creative means
are the instrumentalities of wit and amplification. Its end is to dis-
close, through dynamic interplay of the reciprocal rhetorics of
incision and proliferation, the submerged realities of experience.
Through implosion and explosion of the facts and patterns of common life, it intends to force a new vision upon the reader — to
transform him, galvanize him, free him to become the vehicle of
apocalypse. It is predictable that an imagination so metaphysically
ambitious as Mailer's should generate fictions which, though open-
ended and loosely shaped, contain a dense internal unity of inter-
locking analogies, and that that unity should be mirrored in a prose
coordinately dense with analogizing metaphor.

Mailer's style of imagination is a *forcing* style: it exerts *force*
upon reality; it seeks to *force* reality into the matrix of an idio-
syncratic vision. This *urgency* is the key to Mailer's most prominent strengths: the relentless energy of desperation which makes *An
American Dream* a single breathless action, and gathers the many

moods and modes of *Advertisements* into a sharply unified por-
trait of the artist as a young man fighting the demons of crack-up;
the monumentality of certain of his chief theme-bearing characters — John F. Kennedy and Herman Teppis, Sonny Liston and
Deborah Kelly Rojack — who remain in the memory as vivid
larger-than-life creatures of myth; and the fluency everywhere,
from the close, sharp lash of the goading scatologist to the barrel-
toned magniloquence of the bard.

But these strengths are shadowed by related weaknesses: a dull-
ing of awareness through a persistence in urgency that is too relentless; a flatness, stockness, vagueness in characterization often,
when the fictionist in the author inevitably capitulates to the di-
dact; and a tendency to flatulence, garrulousness, clotted heaviness,
that threatens to choke the naturally vigorous life of the prose.
One is irritated, and finally deafened, by the sado-masochistic
acid-head bebop and chowder mannerisms of D. J. Jethroe's non-
stop answer to the question Why Are We in Vietnam? — though
there are "good things" in this work, and tightened up it might
have made a memorable short story or novella. Sergius O'Shaugnessy is disastrously vague, and Marion Faye is flat; their central
moral significance in *The Deer Park* is diminished to abstraction
and formula by their failure to be as human as the roundly conceived moral cripples surrounding them in the populous world of
Desert D'Or. (Collie Munshin is a pretty bloom of humanity by
comparison.) And the ingenious dialogues on the metaphysics of
death and excrement in *The Presidential Papers* and *Cannibals
and Christians* are, when all is said and done, overextended and
boring. And boring is, of course, one of the most undesirable things
you can be in the Mailer canon of humane values. These quali-
ties represent a temptation perhaps innate to Mailer's kind of sensi-
bility. In *The Armies of the Night*, for example, he is attracted by
the idea of "a short novel about a young American leading a double

life in college as a secret policeman." Such a novel might be somewhat less vulnerable to prefabricated literary patterning than *Vietnam* (father-son tensions, heterosexual-homosexual tensions, man-beast tensions, all framed in a "significant" Texas-Alaska polar symbology); but even so it would threaten to become an "idea for a novel novel" (a useful phrase adapted from Donald Hall) — something quite "made up" and possibly *forced.*

Toward the end of *The Armies of the Night*, Mailer writes of his feelings upon his release from jail after the demonstrations in Washington: "yes, in this resumption of the open air after twenty-four hours, no more, there was a sweet clean edge to the core of the substance of things — *a monumentally abstract remark which may be saved by the concrete observation* that the air was good in his lungs . . . [my italics]." The bard, perhaps wearied by labor too large and prolonged, has mauled a small bright human fact with the dull brutality of abstraction; and "Mailer," throwing off the robes of office, rebukes his alter ego for this crime against nature.

Mailer once wrote a story called "The Paper House," one of the conventionally "realistic" stories of the early 1950's that he does not take very seriously now, which is all about how reality takes its vengeance upon the criminal abstractionist. The setting is Japan. An arrogant, boorish, and selfish G.I. named Hayes is unsparingly loved by Yuriko, a geisha uncommonly endowed with dignity as well as tenderness. By night he nourishes upon her love. By day he is the thorough cynic: "crap" is what he calls the unhappy story of her family's misfortunes, her indenturing to training and service, and her final and staunch pride in earning the status of "first-class geisha." Crap: she is a common whore. He subconsciously wants to marry her, the natural concomitant in him of her unqualified love. But instead he drunkenly jeers at her: she is a common whore, and he will return to the States without her. When

she responds by claiming him with increased vigor he strikes and
strips her, brutally humiliating her before her peers and their
clients. Later, when he meekly returns, she is as warm with him as
ever, but sad and a bit withdrawn. What does this mean? She must
go on a journey very soon, somewhat before his own departure for
the States. Where? he persists. Why? What sort of journey? Finally
he learns: because she, a first-class geisha, has been publicly dis-
honored by her lover, she will commit hari-kari. Crap! he cries in
irritable disdain. He will speak no more of it. A whore is a whore!
But through the days that follow, her familiar tender attentions
are touched with silent grief. Though he does not deign to speak
of her threat, inside he aches with dread. And on the appointed day
he cannot hold himself back from going to her. He finds her dressed
in white, "without ornament, and without makeup," pleased that
he has come after all to say "Bye-bye." As she turns to go to her
self-appointed justice, he catches her by the arm, crying, "You
got to stop this. It's crap." "Crap-crap," says Yuriko in answer,
giggling. And hidden all around, the other geishas echo, "Crap-
crap." Hayes retreats, and the girls follow him, a massed march of
laughing, bright-kimonoed angels of derision jeering the conquered bully through the town to the chorused tune of "Crap-crap,
Crap-crap."

A memorably fine story in its own right (Mailer acknowledges
indebtedness to Vance Bourjaily for the anecdote on which it is
based) , it is also a model of Mailer's vision of marriage (in the soul-
dimension Hayes and Yuriko are already "married") as the ultimate
battleground of the laws of strife that govern love and sexuality,
and in turn all of life. Alternatively turned on its side, up-
ended, and inverted, "The Paper House" becomes a paradigm of
the love-as-soulmaking-or-soulbreaking-combat themes of *The
Deer Park*, "The Time of Her Time," and *An American Dream*.
But it can also be read as a paradigm of the larger operations of

37

a yet more ultimate law. In sharp contrast to his tender and humane buddy who narrates the story, Hayes is terrified of empathy. His is the naturally totalitarian temperament, bellowing, pounding, *forcing* reality to the shape of his belief. But Yuriko, whose unreasoning love frightens him into his worst brutality, *is* reality. The dignity of her otherness will not bend; she will not, finally, be forced. Her suavely just humiliation of her lover is so satisfying because it is a *natural* justice. A perfect illustration of the penalties which in the natural scheme of things are levied against unrepentant abstractionists who sin, through violence or neglect, against the actual.

This formula may provide one explanation of why it is that some people "can't read" Mailer any more, and why even those who can and do read him find themselves at times, especially when reading his fiction, fatigued, irritated, hankering after something which the apocalyptic apparatus of his imagination quite purposely extracts and draws off from his material so that no dilution will threaten the strong potion of his vision. Perhaps it is thanks to the just and beneficent workings of Yuriko's law that Mailer cannot finally succeed in this effort. Perhaps this explains why his best work, the work that moves as well as amazes, is his most "impure" — as in *The Deer Park*, where the mere presence of Charles Francis Eitel and Elena Esposito mocks, with the awesome poignant reality of their flawed selves and failed love, the unreality of Sergius O'Shaugnessy and Marion Faye, those stiff and faceless standard-bearers of the author's abstract redemptive "truth."

While Mailer has steadfastly refused to be apologetic about his journalism, he has equally steadfastly identified his highest goals as a writer with some major achievement as a novelist. In *The Armies of the Night* he is quite openly if good-humoredly annoyed by Robert Lowell's insistent praises of him as our greatest "journalist" at the same time he envies Lowell's quiet authority in the role of "poet." It is a fact, I think, that the large and responsive audience Mailer has now won at the close of the sixties would tend to agree, no doubt to the writer's chagrin, that his "best" work has been in nonfiction. In putting forth my own concurrence I would want to make clear that while I view *Barbary Shore* and *Why Are We in Vietnam?* as inferior achievements (they are "abstract" in my sense of the word: they busy themselves making points rather than peopling a world; and the mannerisms of their prose, portentous in one case, ranting in the other, are dubious compensation for this impoverishment) they nevertheless have interest and deserve respect in the total picture of Mailer's career as honorable attempts at experiment and innovation.

Granting the solid excellence — its truth of substance and feeling, as well as its art — of *The Naked and the Dead,* and the breathless virtuosity of *An American Dream,* only *The Deer Park* remains in the running for honors as a "great" novel. Its depth and breadth of imaginative engagement with our time, its acute and inclusive sensing of the way we live now, through deft selection of setting and symbol and deft portraiture of a dozen varied secondary characters that are real as well as symptomatic, make it impressive. But as we move toward the core of this book — the affair between Elena and Eitel — surely we move from the impressive into the field of force of something like "greatness." Eitel, the hero-gentleman demeaned by history, is a complex character of almost tangible reality; he has all the fullness of being that Fitzgerald could not finally give to Dick Diver. Elena, the soiled broad and dumb waif of petty disasters, is rich with an inner gift of instinctive warmth and natural dignity worthy of Cleopatra; she is one of the few great woman characters in American fiction after James. The delicate, tender persistence of Mailer's articulation of the life of their affair, its growth, flowering, deterioration, and crippled resolution, is rare and magnificent. It is the *real*

39

"armature" of the book, despite Mailer's efforts to give that power to his prophets of new consciousness, Marion Faye and Sergius O'Shaugnessy. Because Sergius, like Lovett in *Barbary Shore*, seems neither intelligent nor sensitive nor good enough, nor even *visible* enough, to attract the friendship and confidence of a man like Eitel, we do not believe in him. But we cannot quite console ourselves by saying, with Lawrence, "Never trust the author, trust the tale," because we are distracted and fatigued as we read by the badgering of Mailer's forcing style of imagination — and the book's armature slows, finally, and falters. *The Deer Park*, one can say (Mailer's exactly opposite account of its shortcomings notwithstanding), was a potentially great novel flawed by an authorial excess of misled good intentions. It is perhaps yet another validation of Yuriko's law that what remains persistently alive in one's memory of *The Deer Park* is Eitel and Elena, and the real world, intimate and at large, of which they were the vital center.

In the middle 1950's Mailer professed a credo that would still seem to hold for him in the late 1960's:

I suppose that the virtue I should like most to achieve as a writer is to be genuinely disturbing . . . It is, I believe, the highest function a writer may serve, to see life (no matter by what means or form or experiment) as others do not see it, or only partially see it, and therefore open for the reader that literary experience which comes uniquely from the novel — the sense of having one's experience enlarged, one's perceptions deepened, and one's illusions about oneself rendered even more untenable. For me, this is the highest function of art, precisely that it is disturbing, that it does not let man rest, and therefore forces him so far as art may force anything to enlarge the horizons of his life.

It is clear that most of his work to date has been done in the light of this statement of principle, and it seems probable that it will continue to be, if only because it is the kind of principle that any serious novelist of whatever artistic or philosophic persuasion would be likely to subscribe to with dedication. But it could be argued that in his fiction, at least, Mailer has yet to write a book worthy of the strictest interpretation of his principle. If he eventually completes the multi-volume quasi-epic of neo-Joycean structure and Burroughs-*cum*-Tolstoian substance that he has been promising these many years, it probably will not be the novel, any more than his others have been, that fulfills the high aims of this credo. If he is to write a truly "great" novel, it will be the product of some new, subtler, and perhaps unimaginably humbler synthesis of the gifts for which he has now come to be appreciated. Perhaps he will learn something from his readers' obstinate tendency to prefer his nonfiction, where, with no sacrifice of his skills and all benefit to the power of his vision, he is happily mired in reality, hobbled to the facts of time, place, self, as to an indispensable spouse of flesh and blood who continually saves him from his other self that yearns toward wasteful flirtations with *Spiritus Mundi*. In any case, he will have to come to know truly, if in his own way, the "Thou" to which the "I" of Martin Buber's world is inexorably wedded, and he will have to find his own style of that "negative capability" which Keats identified as the root of true imagination.

Perhaps Mailer would dismiss such cavils as typical of the solemnly moribund mentality of official literary criticism. And yet he might be reminded that the newly respectful concern with his work, represented even by such exceptions as these, is the natural harvest, sought or not, of his maverick persistence in his calling — and for Mailer writing has always been, literally, a "calling" — despite the years of criticism's ignorant undervaluation of him. He has finally forced criticism, which once dismissed him as a sensationalist barbarian egomaniac who couldn't write, to eat its own words, salted and spiced with the true savor of his actual achievements. Criticism has been made to confess at last that Mailer is a symbolist and mythmaker, the alchemy of his imagination being capable of turning excrement, madness, and perversion into lambent revelations of the condition of man and God; that he is a true intellectual — acute, sophisticated, and dead serious in his probing criticisms of the life of his time; that he is an extraordinary prose stylist in the big-voiced Amercan tradition of Melville and Faulkner; and that he is fortunately endowed, as most apocalyptics are not, with the easing human graces of wit and humor. Even such a book as *Advertisements for Myself,* which at the time of its publication so outraged and embarrassed the critics with its naked revelations of its author's wounds and vanities, has now come to seem, in the manner of Fitzgerald's "Crack-Up" essays, a nobly original undertaking of self-definition, moving in content and daring in execution. *Advertisements* represents the invention, furthermore, of a new form (let's call it, to borrow a current term that has been misapplied elsewhere, the "nonfiction novel"), a form that has since served him well in *The Presidential Papers, Cannibals and Christians,* and *The Armies of the Night,* and will no doubt continue to do so.

But if his readers continue to feel, with some validity, that in the light of "the tradition" Mailer is not the finished and fully responsible writer-as-*artist* that many of his peers are, it has become easier lately to answer with equal validity that he nevertheless satisfies again and again, as they do not, by surprise. Where critics once measured his failings by the more finished accomplishments of his peers, it is now possible to suggest measurement of the shortcomings of his peers by citing the obstinate vigor of Mailer's restless creativity. For example: we are now capable of thinking (however our words are chosen to express the thought) of Mailer's imaginative ingenuity, that it is never so depthless as Barth's can be; of his ambitious fluency of expression, that it is never so hollow and self-serving as Styron's penchant for "style" can become; of his ideas and his humanity, that they do not seem borrowed or "literary" as do, respectively, a large portion of Bellow's and Malamud's.

It may be that Mailer has succeeded in enlarging a little the range of literature in his time, and that in so doing he has measurably modified our view of "the tradition." What is at least certain is that simply by persisting in being what he must be, writing as he must write, he has taught many of his critics to think more justly about his work, to respond more accurately to it. And a friendly commentator, taking all these facts and speculations into account, could hope that the work Mailer does in the future will fully justify what a young English instructor, whose equivalent only a few years ago would have turned the corners of his mouth down at the mere mention of Mailer's name, said to me only days before these sentences were written — "He's about the best we've got going for us now."

↙ Selected Bibliography

Works of Norman Mailer

NOVELS AND COLLECTIONS OF SHORT STORIES

The Naked and the Dead. New York: Holt, Rinehart, and Winston, 1948.
Barbary Shore. New York: Holt, Rinehart, and Winston, 1951.
The Deer Park. New York: Putnam, 1955; Dial, 1967.
An American Dream. New York: Dial, 1965.
The Short Fiction of Norman Mailer. New York: Dell (paperback), 1967.
Why Are We in Vietnam? New York: Putnam, 1967.

OTHER PROSE

Advertisements for Myself. New York: Putnam, 1959.
The Presidential Papers. New York: Putnam, 1963.
Cannibals and Christians. New York: Dial, 1966.
The Armies of the Night. New York: New American Library, 1968.
The Bullfight, a Photographic Narrative with Text by Norman Mailer. New York: CBS Legacy Collection Book, distributed by Macmillan, 1967.

PLAY

The Deer Park. New York: Dial, 1967.

POEMS

Deaths for the Ladies, and Other Disasters. New York: Putnam, 1962.

CURRENT AMERICAN REPRINTS

Advertisements for Myself. New York: Berkley. $.95.
An American Dream. New York: Dell. $.95.
Barbary Shore, with Introduction by Norman Podhoretz. New York: Universal Library (Grosset). $1.95. New York: Signet (New American Library). $.75.
Cannibals and Christians. New York: Dell. $.95.
The Deer Park. New York: Berkley. $.75. New York: Signet. $.75.
The Deer Park (play). New York: Dell. $.95.
The Idol and the Octopus (original). New York: Dell. $.95.
The Naked and the Dead. New York: Signet. $.95. New York: Holt, Rinehart,

44

and Winston (edited by Chester E. Eisinger). $2.95. New York: Modern Library (Random House). $2.45.

The Short Fiction of Norman Mailer (original). New York: Dell. $.95.

The White Negro (original). San Francisco: City Lights Book Shop. $.75.

Why Are We in Vietnam? New York: Berkley. $.95.

Critical and Biographical Material

Aldridge, John W. *Time to Murder and Create.* New York: McKay, 1966.

Blotner, Joseph. *The Political Novel in America.* Austin and London: University of Texas Press, 1966.

Breit, Harvey. *The Writer Observed.* Cleveland and New York: World, 1956.

Corrington, J. W. "An American Dream," *Chicago Review,* 18:58–66 (Summer 1965).

Dienstfrey, Harris. "Norman Mailer," in *On Contemporary Literature,* edited by Richard Kostelanetz. New York: Avon, 1964.

Eisinger, Chester E. *Fiction of the Fifties.* Chicago: University of Chicago Press, 1963.

Glicksberg, Charles I. "Norman Mailer: The Angry Young Novelist in America," *Wisconsin Studies in Contemporary Literature,* 1:25–34 (Winter 1960).

Harper, Howard M., Jr. *Desperate Faith.* Chapel Hill: University of North Carolina Press, 1967.

Hoffman, Frederick J. "Norman Mailer and the Heart of the Ego: Some Observations on Recent American Literature," *Wisconsin Studies in Contemporary Literature,* 1:5–12 (Fall 1960).

Ludwig, Jack. *Recent American Novelists.* Minneapolis: University of Minnesota Press, 1962.

Millgate, Michael. *American Social Fiction: James to Cozzens.* Edinburgh and London: Oliver and Boyd, 1964.

"Norman Mailer: An Interview," in *Writers at Work: The Paris Review Interviews* (third series), with Introduction by Alfred Kazin. New York: Viking, 1967.

"*Playboy* Interview: Norman Mailer," *Playboy,* 15:69–84 (January 1968).

Podhoretz, Norman. "Norman Mailer: The Embattled Vision," *Partisan Review,* 26:371–91 (Summer 1959).

Poirier, Richard. "T. S. Eliot and the Literature of Waste," *New Republic,* 156:19–25 (May 20, 1967).

Schrader, George A. "Norman Mailer and the Despair of Defiance," *Yale Review,* 51:267–80 (Winter 1962).

Toback, James. "Norman Mailer Today," *Commentary,* 44:68–76 (October 1967).

Schulz, Max F. "Mailer's Divine Comedy," *Contemporary Literature*, 9:36–57 (Winter 1968).

Trilling, Diana. "The Radical Moralism of Norman Mailer," in *The Creative Present*, edited by Nona Balakian and Charles Simmons. Garden City, N.Y.: Doubleday, 1963.

Volpe, Edmund L. "James Jones — Norman Mailer," in *Contemporary American Novelists*, edited by Harry T. Moore. Carbondale: Southern Illinois University Press, 1964.

Wagenheim, Allen J. "Square's Progress: *An American Dream*," *Critique*, 10:45–68 (Winter 1968).

Weber, Brom. "A Fear of Dying: Norman Mailer's *An American Dream*," *Hollins Critic*, 2:1–6 (1965).

Wood, Margery. "Norman Mailer and Nathalie Sarraute: A Comparison of Existentialist Novels," *Minnesota Review*, 6:67–72 (Spring 1966).

VITAL ISSUES IN MODERN ARMENIAN HISTORY

*A Documented Exposé of Misrepresentations
in Turkish Historiography*

by

E. K. SARKISIAN AND R. G. SAHAKIAN
ARMENIAN ACADEMY OF SCIENCES, EREVAN

Translated and Edited
With an Introduction, Maps and Postscript

by

ELISHA B. CHRAKIAN

ARMENIAN STUDIES
P. O. Box 119
WATERTOWN, MASSACHUSETTS

Price Three Dollars

1 9 6 5

Library of Congress Catalog Card No. 65-19371

A publication of Library of Armenian Studies, P. O. Box 119, Watertown, Massachusetts 02172.

Vital Issues in Modern Armenian History: A Documented Exposé of Misrepresentations in Turkish Historiography is a translation (edited) of the Armenian text: Ervant K. Sarkisian and Ruben G. Sahakian, *Hai Djoghovourtie Nor Shurtchanie Badmouthian Nenkapokhoume Tourk Badmakrouthian Metch.* Erevan, Armenian SSR., Haibedhrad, 1963.

PRINTED BY THE CONCORD PRESS, WEST CONCORD, MASSACHUSETTS
UNITED STATES OF AMERICA

1915 - April 24 - 1965

It is rather for us to be dedicated to the great task remaining before us — that from these honored dead we take increased devotion to that cause for which they gave the last measure of devotion; that we here highly resolve that these dead shall not have died in vain. . . .

Abraham Lincoln on November 19, 1863, at Gettysburg National Cemetery.

The issuance in English of this work by me coincides with this year's worldwide commemoration by Armenians of the fiftieth anniversary of that all-encompassing Tragedy that befell their kin in Turkey during World War I. I, therefore, offer it in reverent remembrance of the myriad innocent victims of that Turkish Genocide of my forebears and of the selfless, martyred, champions of the concept of the intrinsic worth and dignity of man, as man, and of the welfare and freedom of this once oppressed and decimated people.

EBC

CONTENTS

INTRODUCTION
by E. B. Chrakian

THIS STUDY, by two senior members of the Armenian Academy of Sciences, is at once a review and an exposé, based on published documentary evidence, hitherto untapped archives, and other relevant source-materials, both indigenous and otherwise, of the perfidious distortions of the nature and import of a number of crucial matters involving, in particular, recent Armenian history, that are advanced and promoted in our times by Turkish memorialists, political and military writers, and historians.

For instance, it exposes the mendacious, albeit quite silly and naive, claims by Kemalist leaders and writers, to territories acknowledgedly steeped in Armenian history and tradition—still part of Turkey today — as *aboriginally* Turkish, on ostensibly archaeological-ethnographic grounds; their unconscionable efforts to make light of, or to explain away, or even to vindicate, the genocidal policies and their unrelenting implementation by Sultan Hamid in the nineteenth century and by the Young Turks in our own, as "absolute necessities" for the safety of the state . . .; their distorted accounts of the total Armenian population and its comparative strength and distribution in the country, prior to and during the period of the 1915–1918 wholesale liquidation, pillage, and deportations perpetrated by the Ittihad-Young Turks.

It explores the history of Young Turk-Kemalist schemes to destroy as well the newly established Armenian Republic of 1918–1920 in Transcaucasia, on territory referred to at times as "Russian" or "Eastern" Armenia; their well-planned invasion of it to that end; and the ensuing characteristically wanton butchery and destruction in occupied areas — in Kars, Ardahan, Alexandropol, and so on.

It appraises the misinterpretations and the subterfuges employed by the Turks in the course of a variety of negotiations, specially those connected with the political fate of Armenia, both pre-Soviet and Soviet, as well as the devious tactics employed to circumvent agreements and treaties, such as, Brest-Litovsk, Alexandropol, Kars, Moscow.

And, in addition to other inquiries into similar abject practices in cognate areas found in modern Turkish historiography, the authors, in conclusion, also call attention to the widespread pernicious influences of an aggressive Pan-Turkism, nurtured directly or indirectly by Kemalists, and its dangers not only to minority elements and neighboring peoples, but to the peace of the world as well.

For the informed and the humane, no unconscionable distortion of the facts of history can cover up or justify in any sense the sheer bestiality of the extermination and of the uprooting of an entire people—on the whole, to all intents and purposes, an orderly and industrious people — as in the Genocide of the Armenians in 1915–1920 by Young Turks and Kemalists, in a sense, the dénouement of a series of acts of collective despoliation and carnage, begun in the third quarter of the nineteenth century. Thus, the boundless, fathomless grief, in 1917, of the poet* of this people's joys and sorrows:

> Bitter, vexed,
> Day and night
> Cureless hurt
> In my heart.
>
> Paternal hearth
> Ravaged, ruined,
> Bathed in blood,
> Sorrows untold.
>
> Blessed tots,
> Mothers, sisters,
> Hurled unto fire,
> Rapier, rivers.
>
> Grief, grief . . .
> So much grief:
> How can I bear
> So much grief?

No scouring, in private or in public, of the fiendish souls and hands of unrepentant criminals and their equally unrepentant apologists, in certain instances indistinguishable, can wash away layers upon layers of the blood of their countless innocent victims, — their hands and souls . . . "would rather the multitudinous seas incarnadine, making the green one red".

*Avedik Issahakian (1875–1957). Trans. my own.

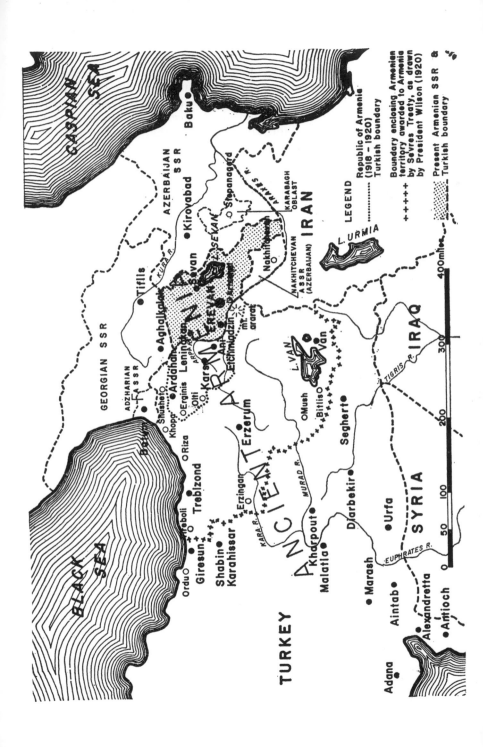

CASPIAN SEA

BLACK SEA

TURKEY

GEORGIAN S S R

ADZHARIAN S S R

AZERBAIJAN S S R

NAKHITCHEVAN A S S R (AZERBAIJAN)

KARABAGH OBLAST

IRAN

IRAQ

SYRIA

ANCIENT ARMENIA

Baku

Kirovabad

Tiflis

L. SEVAN

Sevan

Aghalkalak

Stepanagerd

Nakhitchevan

L. URMIA

Batum

Orduo

Ardahan

Khopa

Shusha

Ardahan

Ardanuj

Erginis

Otli

Riza

Treblzond

Giresun

Ozurgeti

Shabin Karahissar

Kars

Leninakan

ARPA R.

EREVAN

Ani

Mt. Ararat

Etchmiadzin

Erzingan

Erzerum

KARA R.

MURAD R.

KURA R.

ARAXES R.

L. VAN

Van

Mush

Bitlis

Seghert

TIGRIS R.

Kharpout

Diarbekir

Urfa

EUPHRATES R.

Malatla

Marash

Aintab

Alexandretta

Antioch

Adana

LEGEND

Republic of Armenia (1918 – 1920)
.... Turkish boundary

Boundary enclosing Armenian territory awarded to Armenia by Sèvres Treaty, as drawn by President Wilson (1920)
++++

Present Armenian S S R & Turkish boundary

0   50   100   200   300   400 miles

No forced exodus of a people, as was the case with the Armenian people in Turkey, from their centuries-old hearths — their fatherland, can affect their unquestionable historic and moral right and claim to it, and to their hallowed ancestral treasures, monuments commemorative of the divine in man, that are now allowed by the usurpers to disintegrate, or to be desecrated. . . .

No human condition, no human order, can long endure, can remain unchallenged for long, that is founded on sheer brute force, chicanry, abnegation of right and fair-play, that "solves" human problems — individual or collective — by total organized liquidation, wherever and whenever men's heart and reason are quick to respond to the ennobling cause of moral justice and its optimum fulfilment in human life.

And as an auspicious first-step, as a guidepost and promise of total ultimate victory of that Right in the furtherance and actualization of the historic just claims of Armenia and Armenians against Turkey, one may surely commence with the implementation of *Wilsonian* Armenia, born of a solemn recognition of those claims, carved out from segments of territories of historic Armenia in Turkey and united with the Armenian Republic of 1918, and duly sanctioned by international agreement—the Peace Treaty of Sèvres of 1920, even if superseded subsequently by the ignominious Lausanne pact. . . .

It is the earnest hope of this writer also that the availability in English of the factual materials herein, culled from sundry sources that are quite inaccessible, for one reason or another, to many — historians and readers in general alike — and the issues discussed, will help correct certain misinterpretations, as well as omissions, *deliberate in certain quarters,* or oversights, bearing on some of the same issues, that have noticeably filtered through and colored some works in English — besides the characteristically notorious apologetics by Turks themselves — on present-day Turkey.

Watertown, Massachusetts
January 1965

1

THE PERVERSE METHODS AND SPIRIT OF TURKISH HISTORIOGRAPHY:

Armenia is "a mere geographic reminiscence".

Young Turk - Kemalists*

DURING THE POST-WORLD WAR I YEARS there has appeared in Turkey a vast literature that deals with problems related to the history of modern Turkey, in particular, that of more recent times. The essential spirit and direction of these historical writings is Turkism, that is, the glorification and idealization of Turkish history — with no regard whatsoever to well-established facts, and with deliberate intent to distort the historically real.

This Turkism eulogizes the Turkish people's "singularly characteristic role" in the evolution and enrichment of world culture, in the light of which claims, it attempts to justify the tyrannical rule of the Sultans of subject peoples and the inhuman chauvinistic treatment by modern Turkey of racial minorities.

The reactionary and fanatical ideology of Turkophilism was formulated and propounded in the early 1930's, when, under the sponsorship and immediate guidance of Moustapha Kemal Ataturk, was founded *The Historical Society of Turkey* in 1931. From that time on this Society, with the continued support of Turkey's ruling circles, has consistently and unflaggingly championed its aims and purposes, the outstanding interpretation of which is this Society's four-volume *History (Tarih)*.

In its pages Turkism essentially reaches the conclusion that the Turks are the world's oldest people, that they alone are responsible for the spread of civilization over the earth, and that they themselves have been the founders of numerous large and small states. For example, we read on the first page of *Tarih's* fourth volume, which treats the history of the Turkish Republic:

> In the history of mankind no other race has founded as many and as
> great states as the Turks have done. The Turks themselves founded

*My own captions throughout; quotations are from direct statements by Turks reproduced in text. (E.B.C.)

11

the great majority of the governments, kingdoms, and empires of Asia and Europe.[1]

But who, really, that is acquainted with the history of peoples does not know that hordes of Osmanli Turks appeared for the first time in Asia Minor in the third decade of the thirteenth century, A.D., and, in the course of time, founded a characteristically "brigand state" in Karahisar, the ominous prototype of others yet to come?*

*On the other hand, Seljuk Turks appear in Armenia no earlier than the first quarter of the eleventh century, A.D. (E.B.C.)

It is not necessary to supply gory details as to how, from the 14th to the 17th centuries, that "brigand state" put many countries to the fire and sword, destroyed the centuries-old statehood of a number of peoples, and spread itself over Asia Minor, Transcaucasia, the Balkans, Northern Africa, the Arabian Peninsula. No matter how assiduously fanatical Turkish historians try to "prove" the "value" of the Turk for world civilization, they can never disprove the notorious fact that Turkish conquests resulted in a marked deterioration and retardation of the cultural-historic development of those peoples who fell under the harsh yoke of Ottoman hegemony. It is for the very purpose of concealing this truth that Turkish writers deliberately misrepresent the history of the peoples of those countries conquered by the Ottoman Turk.

*　　*　　*

In the "scientific" publications of Turkish historians, in textbooks, and in the memoirs of public officials brought to light in recent times, we find marked attention given to numerous issues involving various periods of Armenian history. In addition, there have appeared of late "research" studies solely devoted to the Armenian people, with the apparent two-fold purpose, on the one hand, of distorting and smearing the ancient past and culture of the Armenians, on the other, of justifying the predatory, genocidal policy of Kemalist Turkey. *The Armenians in History and the Armenian Question*[2] by Esat Uras and *How Karabekir Destroyed Armenia*[3] by Cemal Kutay are striking examples.

This interest in Armenian history is to be explained not by any concern for an objective account of the untold sufferings of

---

[1]*Tarih*, Vol. IV: "Turkiye Cumhuriyeti" (Istanbul, 1934), p. 1.
[2]Esat Uras, *Tarihte Ermeniler ve Ermeni Meselesi* (Ankara, 1950).
[3]Cemal Kutay, *Karabekir Ermenistani nasil yok etti?* (Istanbul, 1956).

Western Armenians* under the cruel domination of the Ottoman Turk for centuries, but by their avowed aim to "validate, establish scientifically and historiographically", in other words, to vindicate the barbarous policy of extermination of the Armenians by Turkish governments and officialdom in the past.

Thus in this very spirit and approach, Esat Uras, "studying" in detail Armenian history from the earliest to present times, tries to synthesize the anti-Armenian opinions and sentiments of Turkish civil, political, and military personages and historians, and tries as well to misrepresent, to give a distorted view, of the past and the culture of the Armenian people. With the avowed purpose of "validating" the erroneous idea — with no basis in fact whatsoever! — that the Turks are the oldest inhabitants, that is, the aborigenes of Anatolia, Esat Uras and other exponents of Turkism labor assiduously to prove that, "Anatolia, the cradle of history, has been the motherland *(Anayurt)* of the Turk from time immemorial". With similar mendacious assertions they deny the very existence of historic Armenia in Eastern Anatolia as the fatherland of the Armenian people. Turkish historians naively think that, by omitting all references to *Armenia, Armenian Highlands, Ararat,* and many similar geographical terms and conceptions, they will have thereby eliminated them from the historically real itself — from having actually existed or existing—and as Esat Uras cynically states, "Armenia becomes a mere geographical expression, a reminiscence."[1]

It is necessary to note that the attempts of contemporary Turkish writers to "establish" the "legal" rights of Turkey to Armenian territories, from the viewpoints of history, geography, and law, have precedents. Both historians and public and state officials have made many similar efforts. The "proofs" furnished by present-day historians very closely resemble the "interpretations" of Kiazim Karabekir. When the Kemalist army had invaded and occupied a sizeable portion of Armenia** on November 30, 1920, Kiazim Karabekir Pasha, then Commander of the Eastern Army and head of the Turkish delegation in Alexandropol to negotiate a peace treaty, came forward with an extensive memorandum on the "historic" rights of Turkey to Armenian lands. In it the past of these same territories Karabekir described as follows:

---

[1]Uras, *op. cit.,* p. 11.

*Common Armenian usage denoting Armenia or Armenians in Turkey, as Eastern refers to the same in Russia. (E.B.C.)

**For details of the invasion, etc., see Part V. (E.B.C.)

Regarding their historic status, it is proven that Turanian* races lived in these lands some twenty centuries before the Armenians settled there. The Urartians had a flourishing, resplendent civilization, and *the cuneiform tablets of Van concern not the Armenians, but solely these Turanian races.* . . . Therefore, in the light of archaeology as well, the rights of the Turks to these lands are obvious and proven.[1] (Italics ours.)

In the same unabashed, deceptive vein, Karabekir cited "factual evidence" from the history of the middle ages: "During the period of Turkish domination, when Sultan Arp-Arslan vanquished and captured King Dionysius of Byzantine at Manazkert in the eleventh century, and when he handed Eastern Antolia over to Turkish princes, *they did not meet with any Armenians in this area at the time.* However, they did see Byzantines and Georgians among the fateful defenders of these lands." (Italics ours.)

As a sequel to these allegations, he further asserted that the Armenians immigrated from the Caucasus and Persia in later times.[2] According to Karabekir, therefore, there were no Armenians in the fatherland of the Armenian people — in historic Armenia in the eleventh century. And this at a time when they, the Ottoman Turks themselves, had not yet emigrated from Central Asia and Altai into Asia Minor, where Armenian sovereign statehood had existed from earliest times; and, beginning with the tenth century, Ani and Kars had been capitals of Armenia.

It is just this kind of chauvinistic misrepresentation that is being utilized in the works of present-day Turkish historians.

These historians are also denying in their published works the heroic struggle of the Armenian people for liberation from the heinous rule of the Sultans and for national independence. They attribute the existence of the Armenian Question to Armenian

---

*Claim that Turks are of "Turanian" stock from Turania in Turkestan, Central Asia. (E.B.C.)

[1]Arm. SSR State Central Historical Archives, f. 200, op. 1, d. 866, 1. 117–118. (In Armenian)**

**I have deemed it advisable to give the Armenian sources in English translation throughout the text. On the other hand, the Russian references are simply transliterated, but others, Turkish and French, are kept the same as in the original Armenian text. Also, since specific references to classified archive — materials in both Soviet Armenian and Russian languages employ the same system, I have used the Russian transliteration for the Armenian sources as well. (E.B.C.)

[2]*Ibid.*, 1. 118–119.

ecclesiastical leaders in Constantinople and to the *Huntchakian* and *Dashnagtzakan* "committees",* who, they allege, simply concocted this question with a view to bringing about intervention by foreign powers, thereby threatening the security and independence of Turkey.

It is quite apparent that the aim of such deliberate falsification is to explain away the criminal depredation of Armenians by the Turk as the direct consequence solely of the operations of these "committees". Even in this connection Turkish writers, however crudely, slyly, distort the very nature of the just and single-minded struggle of large segments of the Armenian people in Western Armenia against inhuman Ottoman rule and for national political independence.

Turkish historians not only discuss matters of vital import that encompass the ancient and medieval past of the Armenian people, but the modern era as well, and, in particular, more recent times.

The primary aim of this study is to bring into the open the mendacities perpetrated by contemporary Turkish writers in their treatment of some important and complex issues of modern Armenian history.

---

*The references are to two Armenian groups: *Huntchakian,* after the journal *Huntchak* ("Bell"), published by a number of patriotic Armenian students in Switzerland, and the organ of the Armenian Social Democratic Huntchakian Party, which they founded in 1887, in Geneva.

Dashnagtsakan ("Federationist") or *Dashnag* refers to the Armenian Revolutionary Federation (*Dashnagtsoutiun — Dashnag,* for short) organized in 1890 in Tiflis, Georgia, by young intellectuals, concerned with the plight of their compatriots in Turkey.

The first formally organized but short-lived, politically-oriented group was the *Armenakans* ("Armenists"), founded in the early 1880's in Van, Turkish Armenia. It is named after M. Portoukalian's newspaper "Armenia", published by him in Marseilles. The present Armenian Liberal Democratic Party (*Ramgavar-Azadakan*), organized in 1921 by the union of the former Constitutional Democrats (f. in 1908) and the Reformed *Huntchakists,* who had split still earlier from the mother organization, traces its origin to the *Armenakans.*

No doubt, the times were more than ripe for such organized expressions, however splintered, of the mounting spirit of protest and resistance on the part of the people to continued Turkish misrule and oppression. (E.B.C.)

2

ARMENOCIDE: NOT QUITE TOTAL (1870–1909):
"Crush the jaws that utter the name Armenian."
Sultan and Young Turks

ISSUES INVOLVING THE MOVEMENT for liberation of the Armenian people in Western Armenia, which spread at an accelerated pace in the second half of the nineteenth century, have received wide attention in the works and memoirs of Turkish historians, state and public officials. Turkish writers spare no effort to refute the heroic popular character of the struggle of the Armenian people against the tyrannical rule of the Sultans, and to identify it with "the activities of Dashnag and Huntchakist committees". In this vein, Esat Uras in the work cited above and Ahmet Bedevi Kuran in his voluminous *Revolt Movements and National Strifes in the Ottoman Empire* devote numerous pages to the activities of these "committees", assiduously promoting the idea that, until their appearance in the Ottoman Empire, there had been no anti-Turk popular movement whatever.[1] These writers have gone so far in their falsifying of public records and facts as to attribute to the same "committees" such heroic and glorious pages in the Armenian people's struggle for emancipation as the revolt in 1862 of Zeitoun, the revolt in 1863 of Moush, the revolt in 1865 of Charsanjak, the revolts again, in 1875 and 1884, of Zeitoun. In fact, it is well known that these "committees" had not yet come into existence in the period in question. Long before their appearance the people's struggle against the cruel misrule of the Sultan in the third quarter of the nineteenth century had attained massive proportions and transformed itself into a national — liberation movement.[2]

---

[1]See Eras Uras, *op. cit.*, pp. 443–446; Ahmet Bedevi Kuran, *Osmanli Imparatorlugunda Inkilap haraketleri ve milli mücadele* (Istanbul, 1956), pp. 186–187.

[2]For details, see M. K. Nersesian, *The Struggle for Liberation of the Armenian People Against Turkish Tyranny, 1850–1870:* Erevan, Publication of the Academy of Sciences of the Arm. SSR., 1955; V. K. Meliksetian, *The Revolt of Zeitoun in 1862; Collected Scientific Studies in the Histori-*

16

These movements for independence in Western Armenia continued in the ensuing years. There is incontrovertible evidence that the Sultan's Government, and independently of the struggle of the Armenian masses for freedom, came forward with a specific genocidal program in the early 1870's to implement fully its policy of total extermination of the Armenian people. The barbarous aims of the Ottoman Empire are clearly and cynically stated by the well-known Anglophile, Kiamil Pasha, who in the days of Abdul Hamid was grand vizier for many years. Speaking about the liberation movements of Christian peoples of European Turkey and the intervention of Western powers, he stated:

> . . . If we nurtured snakes in our midst in Europe, we should not repeat the same folly in Asiatic Turkey. The sensible thing to do is to destroy and eliminate any and all elements which may some day give rise to the same danger, afford the opportunity for foreign intervention, and serve as its tool.
>
> Now, today, at least, the interests of England demand that our territories in Asia Minor (we and England not only do not recognize the word Armenia, but must needs crush the very jaws that utter that name) remain free from any foreign intervention and from all possible occasions for such intervention. Therefore, for the sake of that sacred cause — and our right as a sovereign state demands it, too — it is imperative that we exterminate any and all suspicious elements in order to insure our future security. Thus, we must eliminate, leave behind no traces of, that Armenian nation. And to accomplish this task, we are lacking in nothing; we have all the means we need — governors, judges, tax-collectors, police, in short, everything. We can declare a religious war, an easy war — waged against a 'nation' that has no arms, no army, no leadership. . . . And if that Armenian 'nation' is destroyed and if Christian Europe should look for a co-religionist and does not find it in Asiatic Turkey, it will leave us alone. Then we can begin to concern ourselves with internal affairs and reforms.[1]

This monstrous genocidal program of Kaimil Pasha's government was obviously put into operation in the years 1894–1896 when the Ottoman rulers systematically organized a series of extensive massacres. Prof. Dillon, speaking of the wholesale butcheries of the Armenian people during those years, asserts with emphasis:

---

[1] *Trial (Portz), a National and Literary Monthly* (Tiflis, 1879), No. 7–8, pp. 204–205 (Armenian).

---

cal Museum of the Academy of Sciences, No. 2, 1950; *et. cet.* (All in Armenian).

It is already proven that the pillage and massacres of Sassoun is the *deliberately* organized act of the Sublime Porte, an act planned in advance meticulously and executed mercilessly, albeit the terrors perpetrated . . . evinced a feeling of pity even in the hearts of Turkish soldiers.[1]

Source-materials about the Armenian massacres in the 1890's are voluminous. There are numerous memoranda by consuls and ambassadors in Turkey and Russia, as well as by those representing European states, memoirs of contemporaries, appeals of Armenians of Turkish Armenia, and of the Patriarchate of the Armenian Church in Constantinople. The newspapers and periodicals of the times are full of despatches and articles descriptive of the barbarities of the blood-thirsty Abdul Hamid. And, finally, there is a vast literature in Armenian, Russian, and European languages about the massacres. There is no need, therefore, for detailed discussions of this subject. Let it be noted, however, that the massacres perpetrated in the Armenian provinces in 1894–1896 took the lives of 300,000 human beings; that more than 3000 Armenian villages were burned and reduced to ashes; that tens of thousands were forced to flee their native land into all corners of the earth to safeguard life and limb.

Following these butcheries on a massive scale, Turkish authorities then settled the depopulated regions of Western Armenia with Mohammedans from elsewhere. Nor did Constantinople escape the massacres. The Russian military attaché, Colonel Peshkov, reports in a memorandum dated Sept. 22, 1895, a conversation he had on this occasion with representatives of the "Young Turkey" society, in which he writes that special detachments, organized by order of Abdul Hamid and made up of the scum of the populace and of gendarmes, "spearheaded the shameful drive against the life of innocent and unprotected people who had become the victims of Abdul Hamid's cowardice and blood-thirstiness. . . ."

"To everyone participating in these punitive detachments", continues Peshkov, "were promised 20 piastres a day and a free hand to loot and plunder with full guarantee against punishment. . . . There is more! When on August 14, the minister of armed forces, unaware of the arrangements of the palace clique, ordered two companies of soldiers to put a stop to the massacres, he received orders 'not to interfere in the matter' from the Yuldiz (Sultan's

[1]Prof. Em. Dillon, *Polozhenie del v Tureckoj Armenii. Cf.* "Polozhenie armjan v Turcii do vmesatel' stva derzav v. 1895 g" (Collection of articles) (Moscow, 1896), p. 332.

palace—the authors)."[1] It was later reported that some 800 families were destroyed in these massacres.[2] Turkish writers, either consciously suppressing historical evidence or crudely falsifying them, attempt to cover up the monstrous plans of government circles to annihilate once and for all the Armenian people in Western Armenia and, in general, in Turkey as a whole.

Similar efforts to justify the policy of exterminating the Armenians, both by the Sultan and by the Young Turks, were made earlier, in particular in publications during World War I. Of this vintage is *The World War and the Turkish-Armenian Question* by the one-time Turkish ambassador to the United States, Ahmed Rustem Bey, published in 1918 in Switzerland.[3] From beginning to end, the writer justifies the policy of his government toward the Armenians. With no mention whatever of anti-Armenian measures by the Sultan's Government, Rustem Bey tries hoisting the blame for the 1894–96 massacres, and those that followed, on "fanatical mobs", the Kurds, based on "facts" drawn from reports by officials of Czarist Russia.[4] He says: "The perpetrators of all acts of disorderly conduct in the name of Islam in Turkey are the mob and those persons who acted on their own individual initiative, under the impact of fanaticism and lawlessness."[5]

Esat Uras, a contemporary historian, repeats and develops further the deceit of his predecessors.

Speaking of the 1894–1896 depredations, the 1909 butcheries at Adana, and, finally, of the 1915–16 wholesale massacres and deportations well known to the entire world, he shamelessly asserts that nothing of the sort ever happened, that "the accounts of numberless writers about the killings by Turks of 600 thousand, 800 thousand, or even one million Armenians, are not in the least in accord with reality. Each and every one is a fable. On the contrary, the number of Mussulmans killed by the Armenians exceeds those cited above."[6]

Such deceitful pronouncements of Turkish perverters of historical fact cannot in any way refute what is abundantly reported

---

[1]Central' nyj Goudarstvennyj voenno-istoriches-kij arxiv (CGVIA), f. 450, op. 1, d. 113, 1. 55–56.

[2]*Ibid.*

[3]Ahmed Rustem Bey, *La guerre mondiale et la question turco-arménienne* (Berne, 1918).

[4]*Ibid.*, pp. 7–13.

[5]*Ibid.*, p. 7.

[6]Esat Uras, *op. cit.*, p. 617.

in archives, in documentary materials, in the writings of Europeans. All of these sources expose the genocidal policy and acts of Abdul Hamid, the "bloody Sultan", and of his successors, the leaders of the "Young Turks" who pursued the same policy, but on a still larger scale. The platform of the Young Turks aimed, on the one hand, to assimilate the various Mohammedan peoples, on the other, to exterminate, once and for all, Christians within the Ottoman Empire. One of the first implementations of this dastardly policy was the wholesale extermination of law-abiding and peaceful people in the spring of 1909 in Adana and other Cilician cities. The first wave of these bloody events occurred on April 14–16, 1909, during the days of the reactionary revolt in Istanbul. And April 25, that is, the day following the triumphant entry into Istanbul of soldiers led by Young Turks, ushered in still another series of slaughters.

"This second carnage," wrote Mandelstam, translator in the embassy of Czarist Russia in Istanbul, "was more terrifying than the first. The government of the Young Turks tried to absolve itself of all responsibility by concocting the fiction of an Armenian revolt but had to abandon this version of events in the face of the real facts."[1] And Zinovev, the Russian ambassador, reported from Istanbul on May 1, 1909: "The insanities of the Mohammedans in the vilayet of Adana have reached diabolical proportions. Their Christian victims, particularly the Armenians, number some 15,-000.[2] Soldiers despatched by the government, jointly with a fanatical mob of Mohammedans, massacred Christians, "with no regard to sex or age, and pillaged and burned their homes. . . ." "The city of Adana," the report states elsewhere, "no longer exists."[3]

Gibbons, one of the eye-witnesses of the massacres, gives a detailed description of the carnage, and notes specially that Armenians were savagely knifed and shot on the streets, that they were burned alive in houses in which they sought refuge. The marauders spared neither the aged, nor women — not even children. "This massacre was more terrible", concludes the author, "than those in the days of Abdul Hamid."[4]

---

[1]Andre Mandelstam, *Le sort de l'Empire Ottoman* (Lausanne, Paris, 1917), p. 205.
[2]*Arxiv vensnij politiki Rossii (AVPR), f. Politarxiv,* d. 1034, l. 130.
[3]*Ibid.*
[4]Helen Davenport Gibbons, *The Red Rugs of Tarsus* (Paris, 1919), p. 101.

"Those Armenians who had succeeded in escaping the first carnage are now destroyed. Adana has become a veritable inferno." Gibbons writes further on.[1]

Following the example of Adana, the authorities of the city of Tarsus also organized the massacre of Armenians on May 3, accompanied by pillaging and burning. "The massacre of Armenians", reported the Russian ambassador, "has spread to Aleppo, Zeitoun, Marash, Antioch, and Biletjik".[2]

Still another eye-witness testifies that on April 16, 1909, the local authorities of Tarsus distributed arms to specially imported Mohammedan fanatics who invaded the Armenian sectors of the city and embarked on a bloody massacre. "Armenian domiciles were burned . . . people abandoning their burning homes faced firing squads. Very few Armenians were able to survive."[3]

Contemporary Turkish authors, in their efforts to justify the chauvinistic, genocidal policy of the Young Turks, are obviously falsifying the facts of the history of recent times, among them the bloody events of 1909 in Adana. For instance, the Pan-Turkist historian, Esat Uras, brazenly declares that the responsibility of the massacres of Adana rests on the Armenians, who, as he puts it, "tortured the Mohammedans", adding, "the government of the Young Turks is not to blame here".[4] At the same time, this same writer deliberately and severely reduces the number of victims in the Adana massacres, insisting that the total loss involved was one thousand lives.[5]

Like other Turkish historians, Esat Uras intentionally disregards in this matter not only the unquestionably reliable and verified foreign source-materials cited above, but also the unequivocal confessions and crystal-clear revelations of Turkish writers themselves. Thus, while he repeats the deceit that "the Mohammedans were tortured by the Armenians", he passes over in silence the memoirs of Mevlanzade Rifat, one of the leading figures of the

---

[1]*Ibid.*, (quotes from Gibbons are direct translations from the Armenian text. E.B.C.)

[2]AVPR, f. *Politarxiv*, d. 1034, l. 130.

[3]*La voix de l'Arménie* (Jan. 15, 1918), No. 2, p. 67

[4]Esat Uras, *op. cit.*, p. 575.

[5]*Ibid.* It must be further pointed out that Uras here is actually repeating Ahmed Rustem Bey, mentioned earlier, who, with a view to justifying the genocidal policy of the Young Turks, wrote as early as 1918 that the government is not to blame for the 1909 massacre in Adana, which was simply "a fracas, a fight between two elements in Cilicia, the Mohammedans and the Armenians". Ahmed Rustem Bey, *op. cit.*, pp. 30–33.

*Ittihad ve Terakke** party, in which Rifat asserts that *the guilt for the Adana massacres of 1909 rests in truth on the government of the Young Turks.* "Even during the most troubled days of the revolt of March 31, 1909," writes Mevlanzade, "the *Ittihad ve Terakke* party had not forgotten the Armenians. The Adana branch (the local organization of that party), *in compliance with orders from the Central Committee,* had begun preparations for a general massacre in Cilicia, specially in Adana.

"Spreading the word that the Armenians are planning a revolt and are seeking the establishment of an Armenian national home in Cilicia, *they began the campaign to incite the common people against the Armenians.*"[1] (italics ours.)

In his discussion of the causes of the April 25, 1909 massacres in Adana, Mevlanzade straightforwardly says:

"On Sunday, the 25th of April, 1909, *without any apparent reason,* gun shots were heard in the afternoon from the Armenian sector. Armenians engaged in routine business in the market place became panicky. Propagandists of the *Ittihad ve Tirakke* who were on hand assured the frightened Armenians with the words, 'There's nothing to fear', so as to forestall their escape.

The situation became clear to them with the increasing intensity of gunfire. The battalion of Dedeh Aghajie, with no reason whatever, had been ordered to fire on the Armenians."[2] (Italics ours.)

**Union and Progress* (E.B.C.)

[1]Mevlanzade Rifat, *The Dark Folds of the Turkish Revolution* (Beirut, 1938), p. 171. This Armenian text is a translation from the Turkish edition in Arabic symbols of: *Turkiye inkilabinir ic yuzu* (Aleppo, 1929).

[2]*Ibid.,* p. 174.

3

ARMENOCIDE: TOTAL (1915–1918):

"Annihilation to the last man", . . . *men, women, children, and infants.*

Young Turks and Sultan

TURKISH DEBAUCHERS OF HISTORY have made still greater effort to justify the beastly genocidal policy of the Young Turks toward the Armenians, in particular, for the period of World War I.

In their endeavor to "disprove" the fact of large-scale liquidations of Armenians through massacre, they have represented the total Armenian population of Western Armenia and Cilicia at a much lower figure, accompanied by emphatic assertions that the Armenians have never been in the majority in these territories. In this very same manner, Esat Uras knowingly omits consideration of statistical data found in foreign sources, and bases his findings solely on Turkish population figures, which the Sultan's government, prompted by political considerations, had always, and deliberately, reported in reduced numbers.

Utilizing these figures, specially governmental statistics for the years 1911–1912, Esat Uras concludes that the entire Armenian population in the Ottoman Empire numbered 1,161,000, and that "the Armenians never presented a majority in any locality, not even in the vilayets of Bitlis, Van, and Erzerum. In Sivas, where the total Armenian population was the largest, the Mohammedans again outnumbered the Armenians: there were 840,000 Mohammedans as compared to 170,000 Armenians, a mere fifteen percent of the total population. *There was no vilayet, no sanjak, not even a nahieh (province) where Armenians constituted a majority".*[1] (Italics ours.)

Professor Tayyib Gokbilgen, historian, in his *The Beginnings of the National Conflct,* published by the Historical Society of Turkey, likewise finds that "in the entire history of the eastern vilayets constituting the Turkish fatherland (?!) the Armenians

---

[1]Eras, *op. cit.,* pp. 145–147.

23

have from the earliest days presented an insignificant minority".[1]

In another part of the text, where he returns to the problem of numbers of Mohammedans and Armenians in eastern vilayets, he falls into the absurdity of citing data purportedly from "official European statistics", without one single reference to sources.

"Before the War", he writes, "against a population of 4,000,000 Mohammedans, there were only 600,000 Christians here."[2] He considers it to be an unquestionable fact that the Turks constituted a majority in the vilayets of Erzerum and Bitlis, and that in the vilayet of Diarbekir the Armenian population did not even reach five percent, but was actually closer to 3.5.[3]

These numbers are blatantly manufactured falsehoods. In general, they have no relationship whatever to the facts. Let us turn to the evidence at hand to see how and why:

According to data supplied by Jacques de Morgan, there were 2,380,000 Armenians in the Ottoman Empire on the eve of World War I.[4] The Armenian Patriarchate of Constantinople reliably reports a total of 2,666,000, of which 1,630,000 lived in Western Armenia.[5] The American writer, Joseph Guttman, states, on the basis of figures he employs, which it must be pointed out are reduced, that 1,058,000 Armenians lived in Western Armenia.[6] And George Lenzowski, in his discussion of the Armenian massacres, notes that some 2,000,000 were deported.[7] The French renowned journalist, Maurice Pernot, in his *The Turkish Question*, says that the total Armenian population in Turkey reached upwards of 2,500,000.[8] According to the evidence gathered by the French jurist, Rolin Jacquemyns, there were 2,400,000.[9]* And the recently published *Soviet Historical Encyclopedia* cites the figure, 2,500,000, for the period preceding the 1915–1916 massacres.[10]

---

[1]Prof. Tayyib Gokbilgin, *Milli mücadele barslarken.* Mondros mütarekesinden Sivas Kongresine. Birinci Kitap (Türk Tarih Karumu Basimevi, Ankara, 1959), p. 73.

[2]*Ibid.,* p. 114.

[3]*Ibid.*

[4]Jacques de Morgan, *Histoire des peuple armenien* (Paris 1919), p. 297. (Available also in English translation by Ernest F. Barry. E.B.C.)

[5]*Population arménienne de la Turquie, avant le guerre. Statistiques établies par le Patriarchat arménien à Constantinople* (Paris, 1920), p. 9.

[6]Joseph Guttman, *The Beginning of Genocide* (New York, 1948), p. 9.

*Jacquemyns' articles originally appeared in 1887 and 1889 in *Revue le Droit International,* etc. — an authoritative appraisal of official documents, etc. for the years after 1876. (E.B.C.)

Apropos of the relative percentages of ethnic-national groups in the six Armenian vilayets, Turkish writers avoid any distinction between the Turk and other Mohammedan inhabitants in reporting population statistics because of their pan-Islamic program of assimilation and chauvinistic mentality. In other words, Mohammedans are not reported according to ethnic groups. In this manner, they represent the entire Mohammedan population as made up of Turks only, so that they can insist that the Turks are not only in the majority in all the Armenian vilayets, but even in the provinces.

The citation of just a few facts should suffice to expose this deception: In the vilayet of Van, the Armenians numbered 185,000; in the vilayet of Bitlis, 180,000; whereas the Turks were 47,000 and 40,000, respectively. Likewise, in the vilayets of Kharpout and Diarbekir, the Armenians outnumbered the Turks: In the former, there were 168,000 Armenians and 102,000 Turks; in the latter, 105,000 Armenians and 45,000 Turks.[1]

"Notwithstanding the fact that the Sublime Porte had taken measures to re-distribute, to separate, the Armenian population by artificially creating different administrative districts", writes Diev, "in the provinces of Moush, Poulanik, Khulat, the Armenians were 50–60 percent [of the population]; in the vast province of Van, spread along the western shores of Lake Van, 80 percent", and so on.[2]

It is quite apparent the assertions of Turkish historians about the Armenians constituting an insignificant percentage of the population in Western Armenia and their severe reduction in general of the total count of Armenians in the Ottoman Empire, by which they intend concealing the massacre of more than one million Armenians, cannot stand critical scrutiny. In their "objective",

---

[1]*Population arménienne de la Turquie avant la guèrre. Statistiques établies par le Patriarcat arménien de Constantinople* (Paris, 1920), pp. 9–10.

[2]Gr. A. Diev, *Armjanskij vopros v Turcii*. In "Polozhenie armjan v Turcii", etc. *(op. cit.),* p. 399.

---

[7]George Lenzowski, *The Middle East in World Affairs* (New York, 1953), pp. 48–49.

[8]Maurice Pernot, *La question turque* (Paris, 1923), p. 207.

[9]M. G. Rolin-Jacquemyns, *Armenija, armjane, i traktaty*. Trans. from the French. Cf., "Polozhenie armjan b Turcii do vmeshatel' stva derzhav v 1895 godu." (Moscow, 1896), p. 8.

[10]*Sovetskaja istoricheskaja enciklopedia* (Moscow, 1961), Vol. I, p. 748.

"scientific" works, these people utilize extensively the memoirs, published during the last two decades and introduced[1] with lavish praise, by the notorious cutthroats, the executioners of the Armenian people, Kiazim Karabekir Pasha, Talaat, Ali Fuat Pasha (Cebesoy), and others. And this not simply by chance, indeed. For it is impossible for Turkish writers to get any help whatever, in order to vindicate and to corroborate their views, by citing the numerous published "foreign source-materials" supplied by disinterested observers and witnesses, the collections of documentary evidence, or even from the memoirs and factual reports of Turkish officials who held very important positions during the war, and who, to exonerate themselves, expose, however unwillingly, the genocidal policy and operations of the Young Turks against the Armenian people.

The fanatically nationalist and reactionary Hussein Djahit Yaltchen, in his *Introduction* to *The Memoirs of Talaat Pasha,* published in 1946 in Istanbul, notes that the former grand vizier of the Ottoman Empire decided to refute the accusations made against the Young Turks of World War I. "This book", he writes in the *Introduction,* "is the document *(mudafaanamesi)* that vindicates the *Ittihad ve Terakke party."*[2] Yaltchen correctly appraises Talaat's "creative achievement"(!), whose author, having fled to Berlin after the ignominious defeat of the Ottoman Empire, was bent on vindicating, by means foul and heinous, the criminal political actions of the Young Turks and their administration, which he headed with his associates, Enver and Djemal. With deliberate care and consistency, Talaat distorts the policy of the Young Turk government *vis-a-vis* the Armenian question, to which he devotes an entire section. Now, this is understandable. For, having been Minister of Internal Affairs during the World War years (and from

---

[1]Such eulogies and glorifications of sinister political figures of the past are found not only in these *Introductions,* but also in works of a different character: In *The New Turkey,* a collection of lengthy studies by well-known Turkish authors on the history, diplomacy, culture, rights, so on, of Turkey (published lately in Turkey and subsidized by the Rockefeller Fund), we find pages of similar praise devoted to the Young Turk party and its leaders, the notorious "triumvirate", composed of Enver, Talaat, and Djemal. "These three were patriotic, talented and *compassionate* persons"; " *'Ittihad ve Terakke'* was a political party in the democratic sense" . . . Enver Pasha was a hero dedicated to liberty . . .", writes one of the authors, Professor Enver Ziya Karal. See *Yeni Türkiye* (Istanbul, 1959), p. 44.

[2]*Talat pasanin hatiralari* (Istanbul, 1946), p. 1.

1917 on, also, as *Grand Vizier*), he, with the collaboration of Enver,
Djemal, Dr. Nazim, Behayettin Shakir, and some other leaders of
the Young Turks, had formulated and directed with dispatch the
execution of the monstrous plan for the total annihilation of the
Armenian people. In his *Memoirs* Talaat also repeats the fabricated version about rebellions by Armenians:

"No sooner had the War started", he writes, "Armenians re-
volted in the vilayets of Moush, Bitlis, Van."[1] "Forgetting" his own
personal secret orders and numberless secret telegrams about destroying the Armenians to the very last man, and in this manner
solving the Armenian Question once and for all (these charges are
based on documents published by Naim Bey and Mevlanzade),
Talaat shamelessly asserts that, "when the chief staff prepared the
original outline of the law to deport the Armenians", he *"once
again showed his opposition to it"*. (Italics ours.) Talaat Pasha's
primary aim in publishing his memoirs is to absolve the Young
Turk trio of all responsibility for its crimes. He spares no effort to
vindicate the policy of the Ittihads. He characterizes as "unjust"
the death verdict rendered by the military court of Istanbul on
July 6, 1919, against Ittihad ring leaders.[2]* But with apparent primary concern for himself, Enver, and Djemal, he writes unabashedly: "A number of people have not been rightly condemned,
for there is striking evidence demonstrating their innocence."[3]

---

[1]*Ibid.*, p. 63.

[2]This same court, on the same day, had condemned to death, *in absen-
tia*, the former leaders of the defeated Ottoman Empire, Enver, Talaat,
Djemal and Dr. Nazim, for the deportations from the Armenian vilayets
and for the massacres of Armenians.

[3]*Ibid.*, p. 76.

*Neither post-war Turkish governments nor the victorious Entente
undertook either to bring before courts of justice or implement this military court's verdict against some of these Young Turk perpetrators of the
Armenian genocide during World War I. Needless to say, the appropri-
ation by Turks of hundreds of millions of dollars' worth of all kinds of
properties, etc., which the Armenians, massacred or deported to perish
along the way, left behind, also went unchallenged! (Of some two million
Armenians living in Turkey before 1914, the latest available Turkish figures
show that about 50,000 reside in Istanbul, and around 30–40,000 scattered
throughout the interior provinces.)

Of the Ittihad-Young Turk high executioners who found refuge in
Europe and elsewhere, for the most part in disguise, grief- and revenge-
stricken Soghomon Tehlerian, a student in his early '20's, ferreted out and
killed Talaat on a boulevard in Berlin on March 15, 1921, and in daylight,
submitted himself to trial (Dr. Lepsius was a defense witness), and was

It is this very fraud of Talaat Pasha's that supplies the basis for the views of contemporary Turkish historians. For example, Esat Uras vindicates the executioners of the Young Turk clique by quoting from fraudulent documents forged by the Sultan's Government and the Ittihad Party, the aim of which was to confuse public opinion by concealing from the world their criminal actions. Thus this author cites the proclamation by the Sultan's Government on the occasion of the Armenian massacres, which, along with an attempt to "refute" reports spread about them, stated that:

> in order to establish general peace, the Ottoman Government, in keeping with its unlimited sovereign rights, took measures to curb the Armenian revolt movement, *but at no time resorted to massacre.* . . . If certain Armenians have been expelled from areas involved in military operations, this action stems from the legitimate concern of the Sultan's Government to insure its national safety.[1] (Italics ours.)

At the same time, Esat Uras does not conceal his displeasure with the confession, made in a speech on October 19, 1918, by Prime Minister Damad Ferit Pasha, who had replaced the Young Turk triumvirate, wherein Ferit blamed the former government for organizing the Armenian massacres and exposed the leaders of the Young Turks, who had concocted and published a book to conceal their inhuman oppressions.[2]

---

[1]Esat Uras, *op. cit.,* pp. 620–621.

[2]The reference is to a publication by the Young Turk government, in 1916, in Istanbul, entitled, *The Revolt Movement of the Armenian Committees before and after the Proclamation of the Constitution.* It contained fabricated "documents", photographs, population figures, and other fraudulent data.

---

duly exonerated. Tehlerian died in California in 1960. Behayettin Shakir and Djemal Azmie Bey met a similar fate, again in Berlin, in 1922, in the hands of Aram Yerganian and others. Ahmed Djemal was assassinated in Tiflis, Georgia, July 21, 1922. Enver died on August 22, 1922, under somewhat mysterious circumstances during his Pan-Turanian military campaigns in Transcaucasia — in all likelihood, it is suggested, by a Russian Armenian's avenging bullet. Again, Salid Halim was shot on December 6, 1921, in Rome. All others, now living or dead, went scot free. . . .

Had the enlightened conscience of the day effectively met the crying moral issues involved, even these sporadic *vendettas,* born of fathomless grief, frustration, and revenge, might not have been attempted.

While planning the Nazi genocide of Jews, Hitler is quoted as having said with characteristic aplomb and contempt, "Who today recalls the Armenian Massacres?" Who, indeed!

Fortunately for the future of mankind Nazi war criminals are still being called to account, of late by the German people themselves. (E.B.C.)

In the same speech Damad Ferit, referring to the propaganda
theme of this work, namely, that the mass expulsion of one million
Armenians into the Arabian deserts was necessitated by military,
strategic, considerations noted that this account of the matter cannot stand any kind of critical scrutiny. The Prime Minister of the
Sultan was constrained to acknowledge that nothing could justify
the bestialities that were perpetrated, and that "the responsibility
for the deportation of the Armenians rests on the Government of
the day".[1]

Another well-known Turkish historian, Professor Hikmet
Bayuk, in a lengthy, detailed discussion of the Armenian massacres
in his multi-volume *History of the Turkish Revolution,* repeats the
same deceitful assertion by Talaat concerning Armenian revolts.
Bayur reiterates the view that the punitive measures taken by the
Young Turks were the result of Armenian revolts in the Armenian
vilayets, that the Government itself had not, prior to the revolts,
conceived and formulated a policy of massacre, and that, in point
of fact, *it was compelled* to resort to "defensive measures".[2]

The assertions by our enemies of that period regarding the deportation as well as the massacre of Armenians are false. In fact, there
was a general Armenian uprising at a time when the Turkish leadership and army were in a very critical plight,

writes Bayur.[3]

"Who made the first move in all this?" he asks, and replies:
"It is sheer enemy propaganda, the aim of which is to discredit the
Turks severely, that we were predisposed to deport and to destroy
the Armenians without any cause whatever."[4]

This deceitful account of a "general Armenian rebellion",
which was assiduously promoted and circulated by the ruling coter-
ies of the Young Turks, and is by contemporary Turkish historians,
— this wholly false accusation is refuted not only by the testimonies
of eye-witnesses of the massacres, but even by one of the very Young
Turk leaders, by Mevlanzade, himself. In the work cited above he
confesses unequivocally that the massacres organized everywhere
had forced the Armenians in various localities to resort to rebellion for self-defense.[5]

---

[1]See Esat Uras, *op. cit.,* pp. 703–704.
[2]Yusuf Hikmet Bayur, *Türk İnkilabi tarihi,* Cilt III, 1914–1918 genel
savasi, Kisim 3 (Ankara, Türk Tarih Kurumu basimevi, 1957), pp. 3,
5–6, 9.
[3]*Ibid.,* p. 4.
[4]*Ibid.,* pp. 7–8.
[5]Mevlanzade Rifat, *op. cit.,* p. 147.

We find Mandelstam at the time making similar affirmations:

> Notwithstanding the deceitful communications of the Turkish Government, there has been no Armenian revolution or revolt — not in the least. The Armenians took up arms only when they were threatened with massacre.[1]

Now it is quite natural, of course, that during the massacres, Armenians in a number of places, such as, at Van, Shabin Kharahisar, on Musa Dagh, and elsewhere, took up arms in self-defense, and thus made it possible for some to escape the massacres.

In a crass attempt to misrepresent historical evidence, Hikmet Bayur characterizes the great Armenian Tragedy as "a way of suppressing the Armenian revolt".[2] Comparing it with the extermination of Jews by Nazi Germany, he unabashedly concludes that the action taken against the Armenians, namely, the massacres, were not really conducted on any large scale.[3] We generally find Bayur representing the mass deportations and wholesale butcheries of the Armenians as a re-location, dictated solely by strategic reasons:

"The people were re-located in large groups in the vicinities of Aleppo and Diarbekir", he writes. "They were sent by caravan, accompanied by gendarmes; that they had to supply their own food. . . ."[4]

The same writer reiterates obstinately that local and military Turkish authorities in truth "had treated them [the Armenians — authors] in a more or less correct manner", and that only "in the interior provinces, massacres perpetrated by Kurds and auxiliary gendarmes, contagious diseases, want, and fatigue had resulted in the loss of nearly *a half million people*".[5] (Italics ours.)

It is quite apparent that Bayur makes two misrepresentations: He deliberately minimizes the total number of victims, and then insists that the Young Turk government and local authorities are not to blame for the Armenian massacres. There is no doubt, indeed, that the Turkish historian is fully acquainted with the contents of published official documents in European languages about the massacres, the extant statistical data, and numerous other works,

---

[1] A Mandelstam, *op. cit.,* p. 242.

[2] Yusuf Hikmet Bayur, *op. cit.,* p. 6.

[3] A similar comparison is made by Ahmed Rustem Bey, mentioned earlier, who finds that "the excesses" permitted by the Ottoman Empire against Christians "never reached the terrors of the Inquisition and St. Bartholomew's Day"! *Op. cit.,* pp. 6–7.

[4] Y. H. Bayur, *op. cit.,* p. 8.

[5] *Ibid.*

all of which show conclusively that the great Tragedy of 1915 entailed the loss of more than one million people.

The German scientist, Lepsius,* for example, who was in Turkey during World War I at the time of the massacres, and who, with the help of German consulates gathered and later published a vast array of data and documentary evidence on the massacres, finds that the 1915 victims numbered one million.[1] A. Mandelstam, in his reputable work, *The Fate of the Ottoman Empire*, based likewise on information from German consulates (it would not be in the least to the interest of the Germans to exaggerate!), concludes that more than one million were victimized, of which about five hundred thousand were women and children.[2] A number of other writers cite the same figure.[3] The cumulative evidence from these disinterested sources is incontrovertible, and tellingly so!

---

[1] See J. Lepsius, *Deutschland und Armenien* (Potsdam, 1919), p. LXV.

*Dr. Johannes Lepsius 1858–1926), philosopher, theologian, humanitarian, who, in the face of the butchery of Sultan Hamid of over 300,000 of his Armenian subjects in the middle 1890's, dedicated his life from then on to the amelioration of the tragic plight of these people. Of his chief works, we may note: *Le rapport secret sur les massacres d'Armenie*, 1918; *Deutschland und Armenien, 1914–1918*, Potsdam, 1919; *Jesus at the Peace Conference*, 1919. (E.B.C.)

[2] A. Mandelstam, *Le sort de l'Empire Ottoman* (Paris, 1917), p. 408.

[3] See *La cause nationale armeniene. Documents concernant le problème de la liberation de l'Arménie Turque* (Paris, 1945), p. 20; *Sovremennaja Turcija* (Moscow, Izd. Vost. lit-y., 1956), p. 131; BSE., 2nd ed., Vol. III, p. 65; *Sovetskaja istoricheskaja enciklopedia* (Moscow, 1961), Vol. I, p. 748.

4

ARMENOCIDE: TOTAL'S ALLEGED JUSTIFICATION
(1915–1918):
Compassion is "a deadly ailment".
Young Turks and Sultan

LET US NOW CONSIDER BAYUR'S other mendacious assertion: that the Young Turk government was not involved, was not "an accomplice", in the perpetration of the massacres. There is not one single word in his voluminous study about the secret resolutions of the Government and its numerous orders and instructions to local authorities, all of which made it absolutely clear that the Armenian deportations must be systematically and consistently exploited with a view to their ultimate extermination. Furthermore, this Turkish historian, who cites from numerous sources to validate his erroneous conclusions, must surely have been fully acquainted with the secret documents that were published as early as 1920 by Naim Bey and with the memoirs of Mevlanzade Rifat, one of the directors of the Ittihad Central Board.

The memoirs of Naim Bey, who was chief secretary of the Aleppo Committee in charge of affairs involving deported Armenians, appeared in 1920 in London.[1] By virtue of his office, he had access to a series of original copies of very important documents issued by the Young Turk Government and the Ittihad Party on the subject of the deportation and extermination of Armenians.

The other Turkish source is the memoirs of Mevlanzade. These are valuable because the author, as a member of the Central Board of the *Ittihad ve Terakke,* participated in its secret sessions, in one of which, early in 1915, the savage plan to destroy the Armenian people was first formulated.

Describing in detail that meeting, which was presided over by Talaat and attended by Enver, Dr. Nazim, Dr. Behaettin Shakir, Ghara Kemal, Hassan Fehmin, Djavit, and Agha Oghlou Ahmed, Mevlanzade states that the main report was given by Dr. Nazim,

---

[1]*The Memoirs of Naim Bey,* London, 1920. (Reprinted, 1964, in U.S.A. E.B.C.)

the executive secretary of the Young Turk Central Board, in which he said:

> "If we are going to be satisfied with the kind of local massacres that occurred in Adana and other places in 1909 . . . if this purge is not going to be universal and final, instead of good, it will inevitably result in harm. It is imperative that the Armenian people be completely exterminated; that not even one single Armenian be left on our soil; that the name, Armenian, be obliterated. We are now at war; there is no more auspicious occasion than this; the intervention of the great powers and the protests of newspapers will not even be considered; and even if they are, the matter will have become an accomplished fact, and thus closed forever. The procedure this time will be one of total annihilation — it is necessary that not even one single Armenian survive this annihilation. Perhaps some of you might say, to go that far will be bestial—what harm could possibly come from children, the aged, and the infirm that their extermination should also be considered necessary? Only those who are culpable should be punished. . . . I beg of you, gentlemen, don't be so weak and compassionate", continues this cannibal, "that's a deadly ailment."[1]

Following this, in his discourse on the aims and problems of the Young Turk revolution, Dr. Nazim, addressing his fellow-conspirators, asks:

> Why did we have this Revolution? What was our objective? Was it to depose Abdul Hamid's men so that we could fill their positions? . . . I became your brother and comrade in order to vitalize Turkism. I want to see the Turk, and only the Turk, living on this land; I want to see him become his own lord and master on this land. *Let the non-Turkish elements be completely destroyed — no matter what their nationality and religion are. This country must be purged of all non-Turk elements. . . . Pitiful will be our lot, if a total liquidation, a total extermination, is not consummated.*[2] (Italics ours.)

At this same meeting Dr. Behaettin Shakir also confines his comments to the avowed aims of the Young Turk revolution:

> By founding the Ottoman state upon nationalist ideals and for the good of the Turkish nation, we revolutionaries created the present political order. Within our national boundaries we can permit only Turkish progress and prosperity: *We must of necessity clean up our land; we must destroy all harmful and unnatural weeds — all those nationalities that are remnants of olden times.* The aim and policy of our Revolution is just that. . . .[2] (Italics ours.)

Hassan Fehmin, another participant in this secret session, "explains" in turn how the Armenians should be exterminated:

---

[1] Mevlanzade Rifat, *op. cit.,* pp. 159–160.
[2] Mevlanzade Rifat, *op. cit.,* p. 162.

... Total annihilation without leaving behind even one single soul, is legal [right?].... As it has been said, every one shall be destroyed; there shall be no exempting of the aged, the sick, women, and children. I am thinking of an easy method of extermination: we are at war. We can send those young Armenians who can bear arms to the front lines. There, coupled between fire by Russians facing them *and by special forces in their rear dispatched by us for that purpose, we can trap and annihilate them. In the meantime, we can order our faithful adherents to plunder and to liquidate the old and the infirm, women and children, who remain behind in their homes. . . . This seems a suitable method.*¹ (Italics ours.)

Having expressed his approval of this monstrous program to annihilate a whole race, Enver Pasha adds that "the decision as to ways and means of extermination is the responsibility of the executive committee".²

Djavid, another bloodthirsty scoundrel, "affirms" the view in turn that the necessity to exterminate the total Armenian population stems from the nationalist policy of the Government: "The annihilation to the very last man of the Armenians is just as urgent a need from the viewpoint of our national policy, as it is important for the purpose of attaining economic domination by the Turk."³

Mevlanzade then recalls that at the end of that same secret conference, "upon Talaat's instruction, votes were taken and counted. The result indicated unanimity of opinion about exterminating the Armenians to the very last man".⁴

The Ittihad ve Terakke Party recommended that a special organization be set up for carrying out this decision, made up of criminals and murderers under the direction of the 'three-man executive comcittee', composed of Dr. Nazim, Dr. Behaettin Shakir, and the Minister of Education, Shoukrie.⁵

This "three-man executive committee" in its first session discusses in detail the question of the total liquidation of Western Armenians and the methods by which to implement it. Behaettin Shakir is quoted as having said with unusual gravity that the committee "has assumed a very important and serious responsibility, and if we do not fulfill that responsibility as it should be, *if we should leave it only partly fulfilled, like the previous ones,* we shall not be able to escape the vengeance of the Armenians. . . .". Hav-

---

¹*Ibid.,* pp. 164–165.
²*Ibid.,* p. 165.
³*Ibid.,* p. 166.
⁴*Ibid.*
⁵*Ibid.,* p. 148.

ing pointed out the very favorable state of affairs brought about by the war, he "warns" his comrades that "the suitability of this exceptional turn of events must be exploited to the fullest. *Such an opportunity does not present itself every day. . . .".*[1]

This trio, having agreed that "the task of exterminating the Armenians—the unarmed, the hands-tied, the infirm, and the aged Armenians, to the very last one of them is a beastly crime", decide that its execution can be entrusted neither to the army, the militia, the police, nor to the people in general, because this "will spoil the people, who may later turn against us, and even rebel". They then resolve that the executors of that mass slaughter must be hardened inmates of prisons who are incarcerated for homicide and other heinous crimes. When these are freed, the trio can muster from their ranks a select force of some 10 to 12 thousand in less than a month, which they can organize "into detachments of ten, as a minimum, and of fifty at the most, over which they can appoint trustworthy captains, to whose command the men will be subject".[2]

In order to give a complete description of that execrable "plan of execution", proposed by Behaettin Shakir and approved by the "three-man executive committee", let us quote Mevlanzade in full:

> All the cities and towns that have Armenians, and which of these places must be exterminated first, we must decide with the Minister of Internal Affairs, and to each one of these areas we shall dispatch the necessary contingent from these forces. These will await the arrival of Armenian convoys at various suitable points on the road designated by us. Talaat, the Minister of Internal Affairs, in turn will instruct the executive officers in those cities to evacuate, along a designated route to a specified location, all resident Armenians, in groups, twice a day, and under the supervision of the military police — *which action he will explain as necessitated by their being away from the theatre of war.* Upon receiving such an instruction, police officers will gather all the Armenians together and begin sending them off, under guard, in groups at a time, along the specified routes. When they have reached the place where our specially organized corps of *chetehs** are stationed, the guards will hand them over to these *chetehs,* then return. *The chetehs will at once put to death all these Armenians to the very last one,* and, to prevent any ill-effects upon the public health, they will throw them into pits dug in advance, and bury them. *And in this way they will eventually succeed in fully accomplishing the task of total*

---

[1]*Ibid.,* pp. 186–187.
[2]*Ibid.,* pp. 191–193.
*Reference is to the "irregulars" — brigands, in this case, made up of the freed assassins, hoodlums, etc. (E.B.C.)

extermination. The money, jewelry, and other personal belongings found on these Armenians will be distributed among the *chetehs.*[1] (Italics ours.)

In his summary of the deliberations of this session, Dr. Nazim says: "We are then agreed in principle; there is nothing more to discuss. We must see Talaat and start operations."[2]

There was no delay in obtaining Talaat's approval for these methods of execution formulated by the three-man committee: "The minister of internal affairs, Talaat, had given the necessary final instructions[3] to the vilayets for the deportation of Armenians and the central board of *Ittihad ve Terekke* had advised all its branches and the inspectors."[4]

Mevlanzade's memoirs also make plain how meticulously and loyally local authorities carried out this monstrous scheme and the secret orders of the Young Turk government:

Armenians everywhere, without sparing the young and old, the infirm and the aged, and exempting temporarily only those who adopted Islam, were herded together in one place, and deported in groups under military police guard along designated routes.

The *chetehs* of the special corps subject to the 'three-man executive committee' would await the arrival of these convoys of Armenians at designated places, like ravens awaiting corpses.

Exhausted from the hardships of travel on foot, spiritually demoralized, depressed from having been separated from their homes, in which they were born and bred, these pitiful groups, once they reached their destination where *chetehs* were stationed, would be left in their care by the military police escorts, who would then return. . . . In the hands of these monsters, organized as a special corps, these human flocks were subjected to tortures and barbarities beyond imagination and description.[5]

The first-hand material presented by Naim Bey, an important public office-holder, further shows that, simultaneously with submitting Armenians to the depredations of the henchmen of the "special organization" set up for that purpose, the Young Turk government also approved their mass expulsion into the desert of Deir-es-Zor as one of its prized tools of total liquidation. This latter means the government employed with equally, if not more, heartless steadfastness, demanding, as Naim Bey records, that week-

---

[1]*Ibid.,* pp. 194–195.
[2]*Ibid.,* p. 196.
[3]For the full text of this order, cf. *ibid.,* pp. 197–199.
[4]*Ibid.,* p. 197.
[5]*Ibid.,* pp. 199–200.

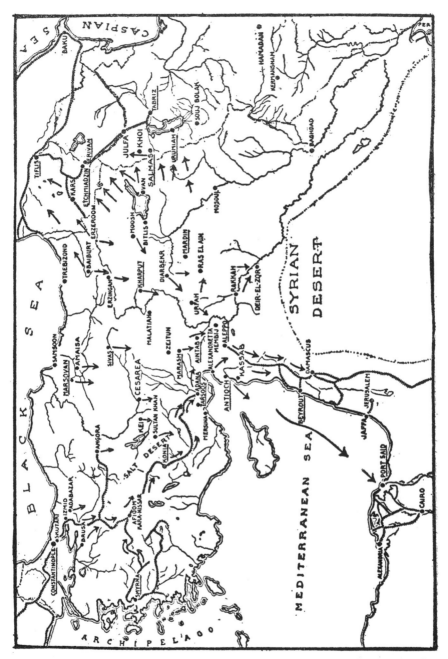

Arrows show direction Armenian deportees from Turkey were forced to follow (April 1915 —). From **The Cry of Armenia,** published by The American Armenian Relief Fund, in cooperation with the American Committee for Armenian and Syrian Relief, New York.

ly reports be made to him on what was accomplished. Whenever word reached Talaat about the mild manner in which some individual Armenians were treated, he immediately sent orders to local authorities not to give way to pity — "to be relentless to the very end, and not to spare even infants in cradles". For instance, in one of the secret orders to the Governor of Aleppo, Talaat writes:

> All the rights of Armenians to live and work on Turkish land are abrogated in full. The responsibility for this is assumed by the Government, which has ordered *that not even infants in cradles be spared.* The results of the execution of this order are apparent in various provinces. Notwithstanding this fact, special treatments are accorded, for reasons unknown to us, to 'certain individuals' who, instead of being exiled directly to the deportation areas, are retained in Aleppo, thereby causing the Government new difficulties. Do not listen to their explanations, or reasoning; send them away, whether they be women or children, *even when they are not able to move.* . . . In place of the indirect means (harshness, haste, hardships of travel, misery, and poverty) used in other areas, *it is feasible to use direct methods with safety.* . . .
>
> Inform those officials who have been designated to do this job, *that they can accomplish our real purpose without fear of being held responsible.* . . .[1] (Italics ours.)

In another secret order, dated September 16, 1915, and likewise sent to the Governor of Aleppo, Talaat says:

> It was previously reported to you that under orders from the *Djemiet* (Central Committee of the Ittihad Party — authors), the Government has decided *to exterminate, to the last man, all the Armenians in Turkey.* Those who are opposed to this order and decision cannot remain in office in the Empire. *Their* (the Armenians' — authors) existence must be ended, *no matter how harsh the means employed may be,* without any consideration whatever for age, sex, and conscience.[2] (Italics ours.)

Following Talaat's instructions, the job of "effecting the death" of Armenians by deportations into the desert was seen through with increasing speed. "The death toll was telegraphed to Istanbul in code every two weeks,"[3] writes Naim Bey. According to his figures, "More than 200,000 Armenians, all those who were convoyed into the desert, lost their lives during the Des-es-Zor massacres."[4]

The Government of the Young Turk party pursued its geno-

---

[1]*The Memoirs of Naim Bey,* p. 16. (Trans. from the Armenian. E.B.C.)
[2]Naim Bey, *ibid.,* p. 64.
[3]*Ibid.,* p. 39.
[4]*Ibid.,* pp. 46–47.

cidal policy with such merciless consistency as to dispatch special orders to pick up and to send into the desert immediately all those children who by sheer accident had survived the massacres. Naim Bey's disclosures of the content of a number of telegrams in code signed by Talaat bring into full view the barbarous, the beastly, character of the Young Turks. Two examples should suffice: In his telegram on November 5, 1915, to the Provincial Governor of Aleppo, Talaat wrote:

> We have been informed that in Sivas, Mamouret-al-Aziz, Dairbekir, and Erzerum, a few Mohammedan families have either adopted or taken as servants little children of Armenians. . . . We hereby order you to gather together all such children in your province and send them to the deportation camps.[1]

In another telegram, sent on January 15, 1916, Talaat stated:

> We have heard that certain newly-opened orphanages are also admitting Armenian children. This is done because our intentions are not known by them. . . . The Government considers the feeding of such children or attempts to prolong their life as acts that are contrary to its aims, because the Government views the life of these children detrimental. I shall arrange so that such children are not admitted to orphanages nor attempts made to found new ones for them.[2]

Of course, there is no doubt that contemporary Turkish "researchers" in history are acquainted with these and similar indigenous documentary and other trustworthy sources. But for Turkish debauchers of historiography it would not help their cause at all to acknowledge their existence. It serves their perverted aims best to call as witness Talaat alone — the arch organizer of the massacres, whose *ad hoc* "explanations" serve as the very basis for their approach and interpretations.

It is in this very manner and spirit, for example, that Hikmet Bayur "has seen fit" to recapitulate the history of the mass slaughter of Armenians in 1915 with Talaat's address, delivered before the infamous last session on November 1, 1918, of the Ittihad conclave.

In that speech, Talaat, pausing over the policy pursued by the Young Turk party with reference to the Armenians, tries in every way to justify atrocities by linking them with an "absolute necessity imposed" upon them solely by the reigning state of war.

Acknowledging that "in all likelihood such a major incident involving deportations has taken place", Talaat, who "has forgotten" his own numerous orders and the secret resolutions of the

---

[1]*Ibid.*, p. 59.
[2]*Ibid.*

Ittihad Government, shamelessly asserts, with regard to the massacres and deportations, that "the Sublime Porte did not act upon
any previously voted decision", and that "the responsibility (for
the massacres, etc.) *first and foremost falls upon the races who promoted intolerable movements*".[1] (Italics ours.) At the same time
Talaat* attempted to hoist the "excesses" permitted during the
Armenian deportations onto individual officials, who "did show
unusual cruelty and violence".[2]

It is this sort of contemptible deceitfulness that supplies the
very premise upon which rests the entire fabric of the pseudo-scientific, the mendacious, approach and interpretations of modern
Turkish historiography in its treatment of the Armenian massacres.

5

ARMENOCIDE: TOTAL AND BEYOND (1919–1920):
"Must needs destroy" this new "cantankerous growth",
THE REPUBLIC OF ARMENIA.
Young Turk - Kemalists

IN THE PUBLISHED WORKS of military and political leaders and historians, in the memoirs of statesmen, in textbooks on recent times,
special attention is given to events of the years 1920–21: to the
foreign policy of Kemalists toward Transcaucasia, the negotiations
of July–August, 1920, in Moscow, the Armenian-Turkish war of
1920, the Alexandropol Treaty, the Kars and Moscow agreements
of 1921, and other related matters — all of which are treated in an
extremely prejudiced, distorted manner. And in anti-Soviet publications Turkish writers spare no effort to justify the Kemalist invasion of Transcaucasia, which they even represent as a "contribu-
tion" to the establishment of the soviet regime there, as being an
integral part of the national-liberationist movement in Turkey, etc.

---

[1]Yusuf Hikmet Bayur, *op. cit.*, pp. 43–44.

[2]*Ibid.*, p. 44.

*Remember also Talaat's boast: "What Hamid could not accomplish
in thirty years, we [Young Turks] achieved in thirty days." (E.B.C.)

The distortions of the aim and nature of historiography by Turkish historians have reached absurd proportions! Chauvinistically inspired "scientific studies" about the most reactionary and fanatical political and military leaders of the not-too-distant past portray these as having played magnificent roles in history. If the memoirs of such notorious executioners of the Armenian people as Talaat Pasha, Kiazim Karabekir, and others appeared in book form within the past two decades, Turkish historians are now devoting individual studies to these same figures in a series under the title of: *The Hidden Pages of the History of the Recent Past*. It is equally characteristic of these publications to dwell also on the issues outlined above in their discussions of Turkish leaders. In this spirit and manner, for example, the well-known Turkish historian, Djemal Kutay, has already published individual studies on Talaat's[1], Enver Pasha's[2] and Kiazim Karabekir's[3] political and military activities. And his venomous *How Karabekir Destroyed Armenia*[4] is representative, in spirit, aims, and method of treatment of issues, of the writings of other historians. This "research study" is of special interest to us because it discloses hitherto unknown data that reveal new facets in the criminal actions of Talaat, Karabekir, and others against the Armenian people.

It is well known that the aggressive intentions and plans of the Young Turks for Transcaucasia during World War I were thwarted by the telling blows of the Russian Army. But the ruling circles of the "New Turkey", resting on the debris of the Ottoman Sultanate, had not resigned from these intentions during the years of the national-liberationist struggles of the Turkish people.[5]

---

[1]Djemal Kutay, *Talaat Pasayi nasil vurdular?* (Istanbul, 1956).

[2]Djemal Kutay, *Atatürk — Enver pasa hadiseleri* (Istanbul, 1956).

[3]Djemal Kutay, *Karabekir Ermenistani nasil yok etti?* (Istanbul, 1956).

[4]*Karabekir Ermenistani nasil yok etti?*

[5]There are even works today that are specially concerned with tracing and describing the "hereditary" ties between the aggressive foreign policy of Kemalists and that of the Young Turks, portraying the former as the immediate successors to and pursuers of the unfulfilled program of the Young Turks. Kutay's *Events Connected with Ataturk and Enver Pasha (Ataturk—Enver pasa hadiseleri, 1956)*, cited above, is an excellent example of this interpretation. The very title reveals the author's aim. Kutay, who is poisonously anti-Soviet, lavishes boundless praise on Pan-Turkism and Pan-Turanism, and points to the genuineness of and the similarity between the ideas and objectives of Enver and Kemal, as revealed also in their personal correspondence which he brings to light in this work (see

The following decision, reached as early as the beginning of 1920, is found recorded in one of the minutes of the meetings of a representative committee headed by Mustapha Kemal: "To dispatch armed forces, officially or otherwise, to the Eastern front, and to undertake the concentration of soldiers in the rear in order to destroy the Caucasian barriers."[1] Kemal himself informed Kiazim Karabekir of this decision in a personal letter, dated February 6, 1920, quoted in *Ataturk in Anatolia* by Terfik Bikilioglu, who is recognized in Turkey as an expert on Soviet-Turkish relations.[2]

It was not, therefore, by mere chance that, although the Greek army was rapidly approaching Ankara, the Kemalists, impelled by their policy of aggrandizement, were concentrating their forces on the Eastern front along the Transcaucasian border. According to Karabekir's own statement, they were to invade Armenia on the "most favorable occasion" that presented itself.[3] It should suffice simply to note that, at the time of the first battle[4] at Inonou, the government of Ankara had only 15,000 men against a Greek force of 60,000, and this when against the Armenian army of 30,000 on the Eastern front the Kemalists had mobilized 50,000.[5]

---

[1]Mustafa Kemal, *Put novoj Turcii,* Vol. III (Moscow, 1934) p. 313.

[2]See his *Atatürk Anadoluda, 1919–1921* (Ankara, 1959), p. 19.

[3]Djemal Kutay, *Karabekir Ermenistani nasil yok etti,* p. 36.

[4]During the battle waged in the environs of Inonou (a village to the west of Ankara) on January 10, 1921, the Turks had 15,000 men against the Greeks' 60,000, notwithstanding the fact that they had already accomplished their aggressive mission against Armenia, and that they could have easily transferred a sizeable segment of their forces to the Eskishehir–Ankara battleline, which had decisive value for the future of Turkey. Yet the Kemalists kept the Eastern Army intact along the Transcaucasian border because of the Kemalist government's aggressive plans for Transcaucasia, her anti-Soviet intentions, and her determination to enforce the plundering Alexandropol agreement.

[5]A. B. Kadishchev, *Intervencija i grazdanskaja vojna v Zakarkaze* (Moscow, Voenizdat, 1961), p. 324.

Op. cit., pp. 27–28, 30–31, 34–36, *et. seq.).* Having identified Enver Pasha as "the creator of the army that carried on the fight for Turkish national liberation in Anatolia" in 1920, he doggedly promotes the view that Enver's anti-Soviet adventure in the Middle East (which Kutay regards as "the struggle for the independence of nations") continued in a different manner the struggle for national liberation in Anatolia *(Ibid.,* pp. 51–52). For Enver's letter, see also: Terfik Biyiklioglu, *Ataturk Anadoluda, 1919–1921* (Ankara, Turk Tarih Kurumu Basimevi, 1959), p. 20.

Even the infamous Enver and Talaat, who had brought the Ottoman Empire to ignominious defeat, and who, disguised, found refuge in Berlin, were well aware of these plans. They even offered advice to the rulers of the "New Turkey", whom they regarded as the successors of their once thwarted policy of aggression. Talaat writes in a letter from Berlin:

"My dearest Karabekir Pasha, if your military preparations are completed, go ahead and attack. *There's no doubt that the victory attained in the East will have a profound influence on the Eastern front as well as on the entire world.*"[1] (Italics ours.)

Relevant also is the fact that, prior to writing to Karabekir, Talaat discusses "the invasion being readied against Armenia" with Enver in Berlin, and receives the latter's complete approval of the project.[2]

It is equally clear from the boastful utterances of the same author that "as early as the months of Spring Karabekir had completed the mobilization and the equipping of his soldiers for the purpose of launching an attack against the Armenians."[3] The following telegram by Karabekir, sent to governing circles in Ankara about the middle of April, likewise attests to the real reasons for concentrating Kemalist forces at the time near Kars and Bayazid: "Very soon now, I shall report that Armenia has been completely erased from the map of the world."

The foreign-language press in Turkey also reported the aggressive intentions and plans of the Kemalists. For instance, the French newspaper, *Le Bosphore,* published in Istanbul, featured a communication on May 5, 1920, from its correspondent in Erzerum "on the existence of a very obvious anti-Armenian disposition in Kemalist circles".

It must be added, however, that these aggressive tendencies and aims of the nationalists were voiced for the first time at their conventions in Erzerum during July 23 to August 6, 1919.[4] To conceal their plans to attack Armenia, they took advantage of the just demands of the Armenian people for Armenian territories by representing them as "combative maneuverings". Thus in a coded telegram on August 3, 1919 (during the Erzerum meeting), Kemal reveals that "the spirit and aims of the Erzerum congress are deter-

[1]Djemal Kutay, *Op. cit.,* p. 27.
[2]*Ibid.,* pp. 25–26.
[3]*Ibid.,* p. 36.
[4]*Re* decisions of this congress, see General Ali Fuat Cebesoy, *Milli Mucadale Hatiralari,* pp. 121–122.

mined by the events in Ismir *and the threats of Armenian offensive action*",[1] which are alleged to be the real causes of the growth and expansion of their national-liberation movement. (Italics ours.)

During the time of the Erzerum congress the focus of attention was not the real dangers threatening Turkey from the imperialist powers, but "the evil intentions of the Armenians".

Furthermore, a specific resolution was passed by the Sivas congress (in session, September 4–11, 1919) committing the nationalists to an implacable campaign against all movements concerned with the founding of an independent Armenia.[2]

In a telegram on November 17, 1919, to Ali Fouat, Moustafa Kemal asserted: "As it is obvious from the decisions of the congresses of Erzerum and Sivas, the nation will not yield even an inch of sod to Armenia".[3]

Under the cloak of similar resolutions the Kemalists were assiduously making plans for aggressive action against Transcaucasia, and especially against Armenia. The question was repeatedly brought up for critical review in the sessions of the Grand National Assembly in Ankara. There is ample documentary evidence in archives of this preoccupation, in one part of which we find stated that the sessions of the Grand National Assembly, with the participation of representatives of the Government in Istanbul,* frequently discussed the question of occupying all of Transcaucasia, took specific, concrete steps to implement it, and sent spies to Transcaucasia and Northern Caucasus.[4]

To carry out its offensive program in the Caucasus, the Ankara government decided to occupy Eastern Armenia on the first suitable occasion. To this end it appointed as commander of the Eastern front Kiazim Karabekir, who had already in World War I dis-

[1]*Ibid.*, pp. 139–140. See also Prof. M. Tayyib Gokbilgin, *Milli Mucadale baslarken. Mondros Mutarekesinden Sivas Kongresine.* Birinci Kitap (Ankara, Turk Tarih Kurumu Basimevi, 1959), p. 168.
[2]*Ibid.*, pp. 167–168.
[3]Mustafa Kemal, *op. cit.*, Vol. II (Moscow, 1932), p. 120.
[4]CGAKA, f. 109, op. 3, d. 298, l. 28.
*Following the dissolution of the Parliament in Istanbul by the Sultan, Kemal set up on the 23rd of April, 1920, the Grand National Assembly in Ankara as the new Government. Thus, there was the Sublime Porte in Istanbul and the Kemalist Assembly in Ankara. It was not until November 1, 1922, that the Grand National Assembly declared the Sultanate abolished, the Grand National Assembly itself sovereign, and all acts of the Sublime Porte, from March 16, 1920 on, null and void. (E.B.C.)

tinguished himself for his Armenocidal activities. Hikmet Bayur confesses in his *Foreign Policy of the Turkish Government* that the government in Ankara was engaged in preparations for an invasion of Armenia for a long time, but that the delay in evacuating British occupation forces had compelled it to postpone action for a time. "Notwithstanding this," writes Bayur, "we completed mobilization of forces in the eastern sector of the country and took the necessary preliminary steps for the creation of the Eastern front."[1]

Mustafa Kemal himself frequently mentions the preliminary preparations for an attack on Armenia. For instance, in an address delivered on August 14, 1920, he states:

> "With regard to the annexation of the three vilayets (the reference is to Kars, Batum, and Ardahan — the authors), the Grand National Assembly has authorized the Council of Ministers to occupy them whenever the opportunity presents itself. To that end, we gave orders on June 6 to the Eastern army to prepare for attack."[2]

Kemal discusses this question in detail in a speech before the Grand National Assembly in 1927. Commenting on the state of events during June of 1920 on the Eastern front, he said:

> "We resolved to invade Armenia. In June of 1920, we ordered that steps be taken to mobilize and concentrate forces in Eastern districts. Kiazim Karabekir Pasha, commander of the 15th Corps, was appointed Commander of the Eastern front."[3]

We find the Ankara Government, therefore, concerned in June of 1920, not with the offensive of the Greek army in Thrace and Anatolia, and its occupation of Adrianople, Ereklin, Brousa, Balikesir and some other cities, not with concentrating its main armed forces on the Western front against the Greeks, but with concentrating them along the Armenian border in preparation for an invasion.

For Kemalist ruling circles the actual existence of an independent Armenia was intolerable, hence their main objective from the very beginning was the extermination of Armenia, after which it would be quite feasible, in their opinion, to continue the fight on the Western front against the Greeks. That they gave paramount significance and priority to their preparations for an offensive against Armenia is amply in evidence in the very interesting data which the Turkish military historian, Chevtath Kerim, presents in

---

[1]Ord. Prof. Yusuf Hikmet Bayur, *Turkiye devletinin dis siyasasi* (Istanbul, 1938), p. 65.
[2]*Atatürkün soylev ve demecleri*, Vol. III (Istanbul, 1945), p. 90.
[3]Mustafa Kemal, *Op. cit.*, Vol. III (Moscow, 1932), p. 117.

his *Lectures on the Turkish Struggle for Independence*. This is what he says:

> "The leaders in Ankara, prompted by political and military considerations, appraised the state of affairs in the East as being more serious. Since the problems involving the wars with the Greeks and the French from the beginning were construed as defensive in character, we, therefore, sought with meager forces to hinder the enemy's future advances with all available means. . . . Our attention was focused on the Eastern front because with the attainment of success here *we must needs destroy the Armenian Army, as well as the Armenian state,* which still fester the body of our country like a cankerous growth. . . ."[1] (Italics ours.)

These matters are now openly discussed by former military officers and historians, among them the well-known historian, Professor Enver Ziya Karal[2], the fanatically reactionary, General Ali Fuat Cebesoy[3], Tahsin Unal[4], who lectures on political history in a military academy, and others.

The cumulative evidence in archival source-materials, the personal revelations by Turkish leaders, among them Mustafa Kemal's, the numerous facts cited by contemporary Turkish writers, unquestionably demonstrate the truth that the Kemalist Government had been making preparations and drawing up a detailed program for a long time for the ultimate destruction of Armenia, and that it undertook the implementation of that program *on its own initiative*.[5]

---

[1] M. Kemal, *Ibid.,* p. 314.

[2] *Turkiye Cumhuriyetti tarihi, 1918–1953* (Istanbul, 1958), p. 97.

[3] *Moskova hatilari* (Istanbul, 1955), p. 61.

[4] *1700 den 1958–e Kadar turk siyasi tarth* (Ankara, 1958), p. 270.

[5] In the light of all this, we think the time has come when we should re-consider the mistaken view, fairly common in our historiography and based on a one-sided evaluation by Stalin as early as 1920 of the Turkish-Armenian War, that "the Dashnags started the war against Turkey" under orders from the Entente (See E. V. Stalin, *Works,* Vol. IV, p. 458). Many writers among us repeat this erroneous interpretation by Stalin and overlook the Kemalists' own specific aggressive policy and concrete plans for destroying Armenia once and for all.

There is no question, of course, that the adventurous character of Dashnag policy was partly instrumental in causing the Turco-Armenian war, that is, its policy of tying the fate of Armenia with the imperialist Entente and of rejecting the offer of aid by Soviet Russia. There are still other writers who link the *aggressive intentions* of the Ankara government exclusively with the political opponents of Kemal. For example, Professor

It must be asserted again that Turks who represent the aggression in the Fall of 1920 against Armenia as the most important prerequisite of the *liberation* movement speak, with no reservation whatever, of the preparations made by Kemalists for war against Armenia, the appointed hour for attack, the concentration of armed forces, and other related matters. In view of this, the confessions of General Ali Fuat Pasha (Cebesoy), a former Kemalist military leader, are quite interesting.

In his memoirs, *On the National Liberation Struggle,* Cebesoy, while discussing in detail the preliminary preparations for an attack on Armenia on the Eastern front, notes with pain that the attack did not take place in the Spring and that it was postponed to some later date:

> "Had not Kaizim Kiarabekir's proposal in May for immediate action against Armenia met with opposition, then in November 1920, when important changes had taken place in the West, the Western front would have been doubly stronger . . ."[1]

In the writer's judgment, the month of May presented "the most favorable" turn of events and conditions for launching the attack:

> For "the Armenian army was occupied with crushing the internal Bolshevik uprisings (the reference is to the revolt in May — authors) in May of 1920 and with holding back the Azerbaijans in the north. Menshevik Georgia was in no position to come to Armenia's aid. And against the Armenians in *that very difficult situation* stood the 15th detachment, made up of three regular divisions and volunteer groups. This force was in a position to defeat the Armenians with dispatch."[2] (Italics ours.)

But why was that attack delayed? Why did it not take place in the Spring? Cebesoy's explanation is that the President (Mus-

---

[1]Ali Fuat Cebesoy, *Milli mucadele hatiralari,* p. 511.
[2]*Ibid.,* p. 485.

A. F. Miller's inaccurate version in *Vsemirnaja istoria (History of the World)*:

> "There were political and military figures in Anatolia who were secret, and even open, enemies of Kemal and who favored compromise with the imperialists. They wanted to divert the Turkish national movement from the fight against imperialist intervention and direct it along chauvinistic lines against the peoples of the Caucasus." (See *Vsemirnaja istoria,* Vol. III (Moscow, Sotekgiz, 1961), p. 452.)

In this manner, the Turkish invasion of Armenia in 1920 was accepted, not as the act of Kemalists but of their political opponents. Such an interpretation contradicts the indisputable truth that the Kemalists themselves in the end followed a chauvinistic course.

tafa Kemal — authors) of the Grand National Assembly and the
Council of Ministers postponed the invasion of Armenia after the
following telegram, signed by President Mustafa Kemal, was sent
to Kiazim Karabekir Pasha:

"Until the decisions of the peace conference regarding us are
made clear, for the present, in view of the course of both internal and
external events, *it is not to our advantage to be deprived of the possibility of coming to an understanding with the Allied Powers.* . . .
The attack on Armenia would furnish an opportunity for the Allied
Powers and America to declare war against us . . ."[1] (Italics ours.)

It is therefore, quite evident from the telegram bearing
Kemal's signature that the Ankara government still hoped to join
the imperialist Allied Powers in concerted actions against the Soviets and for that very reason it was compelled to postpone the
prearranged invasion.

These revelations from present-day Turkish writers, and, generally, the policy pursued by the Kemalists from the very inception
of the Turkish national-liberation struggle tend to confirm the
belief that the Kemalist movement possessed a unique characteristic
that was representative of the Turkish bourgeousie: *On the one
hand, it was anti - imperialist and national - liberationist, aimed
against European imperialism; on the other, that movement itself
assumed an aggressive, imperialistic character in the East with respect to Turkey's neighbors — Transcaucasia and its peoples.* And
this aggressiveness Turkish writers present as an integral part of
their national-liberation movement. There is more: The victory
in the Turco-Armenian War of 1920, which resulted from their
aggressive action, is heralded by these same writers as an important
pre-condition of the subsequent extension of the struggle for emancipation. Witness Professor Enver Ziya Karal in his *History of the
Turkish Republic:*

"The military victory over the Armenians in the East was the
first victory in our fight for independence."[2] (Italics ours.) And
Cemal Kutay ties in the same victory with the future destiny of the
national-liberation struggle: "If Karabekir had not been victorious
in the East, what would have been the fate of the national
struggle?"[3]

Cebesoy gives a similar appraisal. In his memoirs he brings to
light for the first time the contents of a telegram sent to Kiazim

[1]*Ibid.*, p. 482.
[2]Karal, *op. cit.*, p. 97.
[3]Kutay, *Karabekir Ermenistani nasil yok etti?* p. 62.

Karabekir on November 28, 1920, by Ismet Bey,* Kemal's most intimate comrade-in-arms and at the time commander-in-chief of the Western front:

> "My dear, my dearest, brother Kiazim . . . *The Eastern invasion brought life to us and to our cause.* We were so distressed, so hard-pressed, that to begin to breathe again a definitive turning-point was necessary. With the help of the Almighty, you discovered that turning-point both perfectly correctly and successfully . . ." Ismet continues, *"Mustafa Kemal Pasha specially* does not quite know how to express his gratitude. Everyone is repeating the same."[1] (Italics ours.)

With similar concealment of the real reasons and aims of the Turkish invasion of the Fall of 1920, Turkish historians interpret and prize the usurpations of other people's territory, the wholesale extermination of the peaceful populace, the beastly cruelties perpetrated by Kemalist soldiers (about these later) as the fight for "liberation" and "independence"!

---

[1] Cebesoy, *Op. cit.,* pp. 485–486.

*No other than Ismet Inonu (1884–), prime minister, once more, of Turkey since November, 1961. Was chief of staff of Ottoman armies in Yemen and Eastern Thrace in World War I, and Undersecretary of War in 1918. From the outset, closest to Mustafa Kemal, who made him Chief of Staff in May, 1920. Won decisive victory over Greeks in 1921 at battle of Inonu, hence his surname. Made foreign minister by Kemal. Astutely negotiated with the Allied Powers the infamous Lausanne Treaty, signed July 24, 1923 (U. S. Senate did not ratify it), which made a mockery of justice of the ratified Sèrres Peace Treaty of August 10, 1920. (Among other commitments, this had recognized and provided for Armenian territorial rights in their historic homeland in Turkey. *See below.*) Inonu then became Prime Minister as well as Foreign Minister of Nationalist Turkey; "inherited" the presidency upon Ataturk's death in 1938; was elected to that office in 1943, and held it until 1950.

Ismet Inonu may be said to symbolize Young Turk–Ittihad and Kemalist traditions. . . . (E.B.C.)

6

RAPE OF THE ARMENIAN REPUBLIC (1920–1921):
". . . to fulfill our 'national pledge'."
Young Turk - Kemalists

IN ORDER TO JUSTIFY the Kemalist aggression against Armenia, Turkish writers resort to still another device to falsify historical evidence, namely, their attempt to represent Soviet Russia as having approved Turkish aggressive action.

In his Berlin letter to Karabekir quoted above, Talaat Pasha, with a view to encouraging the militarist and antiArmenian predilections of the former, "assures" him that Soviet leaders will not intervene in, will not in any way place obstables before, the advances of Turkish armed forces into Armenia. He writes: "Do not attach any significance to the Bolsheviks being really able to protect Armenia."[1]

But it is well known that the contemplated Turkish attack of June was postponed solely because of Soviet Russian intervention. The communication, on June 3, 1920, of K. V. Tchicherin, the People's Commissar of Foreign Affairs of the RSFSR, to Mustafa Kemal, President of the Grand National Assembly of Turkey, made the position of Soviet Russia toward Armenia and the Armenians very clear. Recalling the promise made in Kemal's letter of April 26 regarding the right of the peoples of Turkish Armenia, Kurdestan, Lazistan, the region of Batum, and Eastern Thrace to determine their own fate, the Soviet Government stated clearly that on the basis of this statement it "naturally assumes that there will be unhampered plebiscites in these territories, participated by emigrants and the exiled who, for reasons beyond their control, were forced to leave their homeland, to which they must be returned."[2] Thus the Soviet government made it clearly known that the future of these areas shall be decided by the people themselves in a peaceful manner, and without any outside interference. At the same time this document serves witness to the fact also that the Soviet

---

[1]Kutay, *op. cit.*, p. 27.
[2]*Documenty vneshnej politiki SSSR*, Vol. II (Moscow, 1958), p. 555.

Government considered feasible, under the conditions made possible by the new regime, the carrying out of the decree of the Soviet of People's Commissars of December 29, 1917, regarding Turkish Armenia.[1]

The Government of Soviet Russia expressed the hope that the new government in Ankara would be loyal to the principles proposed in Kemal's letter of April 26, 1920, one of which was the promise to have Turkish Armenia determine its own fate. In a telegram sent by Tchicherin on July 19, 1920, that dealt with the question of negotiations, it was declared to the minister of foreign affairs of the Dashnag government of Armenia:*

"The friendly relations, which the Soviet Government is trying to bring about with the Turkish national government in Asia Minor, it is, among other things, taking advantage of to obtain adequate land in Asia Minor in order to insure the Armenian people the opportunity for its own development. It was exclusively because of the influence of the peaceful intentions of the Soviet Government that the Turkish Nationalists stopped the mobilization of forces which they had started, the object of which was to strike a new blow against the Armenian people. . . . The Soviet Government will continue to follow this same course of impartial, friendly treatment toward the working masses in every nation. And the Armenian people can rest their hope and faith in its lasting friendly treatment, and within the limits of its power on its aid to prevent any catastrophe that threatens the life of the Armenian people."[2]

---

[1]This resolution, then, reserved the right of Armenians, scattered around the world as a result of the massacres, to return to their country, Turkish Armenia, and to decide the fate of these territories by free and secret ballot. The resolution was not carried out because of predatory aggressive actions taken by sultanist Turkey. This fact is recorded in the collected documents of the USSR, thus: "In February, 1918, by exploiting the incident between Armenian detachments and the Mohammedan population, which they themselves had instigated, the Turks moved their soldiers into the territories of 'Turkish Armenia', and (thereby) deprived the Armenian population of the possibility of applying the right of self-determination provided by the decree of the S.P.C." See *Documenty*, etc., *supra*, Vol. I (Moscow, 1957), p. 712.

[2]*The Great Socialist October Revolution and the Victory of the Soviet Order in Armenia: Collected Documents and Source-Materials* (Erevan, Publication of the Academy of Sciences, Arm. SSR., 1960), p. 353. *(In Armenian.)*

*In the Caucasus, or part of Russian Armenia, declared a Republic on May 30 (28), 1918. Since November 1920, a member of the USSR. (E.B.C.)

The fact that this decisive stand of the Soviet Government compelled Ankara to postpone its planned attack on Armenia is apparent also from a speech made by Kemal before the Grand National Assembly, in which he revealed the contents of the above-mentioned note and called special attention to the irrevocable opposition of the Soviet to Turkey's invasion of Armenia. It was for this reason, he told the *Medjlis* (the Parliament), that they decided on June 20 to stop the preparations for attack on Armenia by the Eastern Army. For the question of the possibility, the feasibility, of an invasion of Armenia cannot be considered in isolation: "Relations with Armenia constitute a small part, only one side, of the total state of things in the East and of the whole network of mutual relationships between Turkey and the Bolshevik Government."[1]

Having accepted Soviet Russia's offer of mediation, Ankara agreed to send to Moscow a special delegation with a view to showing that it was in favor of settling the question of the territories in dispute by peaceful means. In point of fact, however, Kemalists never abandoned their aggressive intentions; they were simply waiting for an opportune time when they could carry on their detailed plans of long standing.

The Turkish delegation, led by the Minister of Foreign Affairs, Bekir Samie Bey, arrived in Moscow on July 19, 1920. It met a number of times with K. V. Tchicherin and his deputy, L. M. Kharakan,* and was received by V. I. Lenin as well. These meetings and negotiations soon demonstrated that the Turkish government did not intend to abide by the principles it had previously accepted as a basis for the solution of territorial questions. Yet Kemal in his letter of April 26, 1920, had ennunciated the main principles of Ankara's foreign policy, which included:

The retention within the boundaries of Turkey of those territories only that were beyond dispute.

The right of national self-determination of Turkish Armenia and of other areas with mixed populations, etc.[2]

On the basis of these principles the Russian Government championed during the Moscow negotiations the determining of

---

[1] *Ataturkin soylev ve demecleri*, Vol. I, pp. 89–90. See also on the same: Ali Fuat Cebesoy, *Siyasi Ratiralari*, "Vatan", Vol. III, no. 14 (1954).

[2] For details see *Dokumenty vneshnej politiki SSSR*, Vol. II (Moscow, 1957), pp. 454–455, p. 725.

*A distinguished Russian Armenian who held various important government posts. (E.B.C.)

national boundaries in the light of the distribution of ethnic populations prior to the world war. Thus it demanded:

"There shall be a rectification of the boundaries of Turkey, such that areas which are predominantly Mohammedan in population shall be included in Turkey, while those territories which had a majority of Armenians up to 1914 shall be annexed to Armenia."[1]

Notwithstanding their former commitments in principle, and because of their aggressive intentions against Armenia, they dismissed forthright the just proposals of the Soviet Government and thereby caused the Moscow negotiations to end in failure.

Ali Fuat Cebesoy, a member of the Moscow delegation and the first ambassador of Kemalist Turkey to Soviet Russia, writing about the negotiations in the summer of 1920 in his *Memoirs in Moscow,* published in 1955, attempts to conceal or deny the aggressive plans of the Ankara Government. His account of the actual state of things is such as to characterize the territorial claims of Ankara as perfectly legitimate and as involving decidedly Turkish lands only. He says:

"The Government of Ankara did not entertain any hostile intentions against neighboring countries, and did not pursue any other aim than the achievement of its independence and freedom *within the areas of its national boundaries."*[2] (Italics ours.)

With characteristic misrepresentations Turkish writers hold the Russian Government responsible for the failure of the Moscow negotiations. This is what Professor Enver Behnan Shapolyo insists on in his *History of the Turkish Republic,* that is, that no agreement was reached in Moscow because of the position taken by the Russians, thereby causing the failure of the negotiations.[3] Similar assertions are made by Mukerren Kamil Su,[4] Professor Esmer,[5] and Tevfik Biyiklioglu, who says:

"The main reason for not ratifying the preliminary agreement for friendly relations signed in Moscow on August 24, 1920, was that the Soviets intended to give territories *encompassing our Eastern vilayets* to the Dashnag Armenians."[6] (Italics ours.)

---

[1]*Op. cit.,* Vol. II, pp. 726–727.
[2]*Moscova hatiralari,* pp. 90–91.
[3]*Turkiye Cumhuriyeti tarihi* (Istanbul, 1954), p. 67.
[4]Mukerrem Kamil Su ve Kamil Su, *Turkiye Cumhuriyeti tarihi* (Istanbul, 1957). pp. 77–78.
[5]Prof. Ahmet Sukru Esmer, *Turk diplomasisi,* 1920–1955, "Yeni Turkiye" (Istanbul, 1959), p. 69.
[6]*Belleten* (Temmuz, 1961), p. 479. Cf. also the same author's *Ataturk Anadoluda* (Ankara, 1959), p. 20.

Then, Biyiklioglu, in the same fraudulent vein, "justifies" the Kemalist invasion of Armenia in the Fall of 1920 by representing it as a peace-promoting action:

"The purpose and end of our military actions against Dashnag Armenia during the brief period of September–October, 1920, was to establish peace and order in that area and to fulfill our 'national pledge'."[1]

What is more, this attack on Armenia, which Kemalist historians represent as a "legitimate" undertaking, did not merely have as its aim the subjugation of Armenia. The attack was at the same time aimed at Soviet Russia, and had all the earmarks of a base anti-Soviet maneuvering which it attempted to conceal. V. I. Lenin saw and wrote about this at the time. In his report on October 9, 1920, *On the Internal and External State of the Republic,* he considered conditions in the Caucasus as involved and complex, and concluded as well that it is likely the Kemalists will not be content with defeating Armenia only: "The Turks commenced their attack on Armenia lately with the intention to occupy Batum, and after that, in all probability, Baku as well."[2]

As to the kind of "peace and order" Kemalist soldiers assured for the areas occupied by them, as a result of the invasion of Armenia in September of 1920, is evident in numerous archival materials and in documents published recently by the ministry of foreign affairs of the USSR. Let us mention some of them:

In one document, which portrays in detail the occupation of Kars by the Turkish army, it was recorded that for two full weeks the peaceful civil population of that city and the surrounding towns was subjected to massacres; that the number of those killed was countless. . . . The same report states that:

"Having captured Kars, the Turks immediately undertook to transport to Sarikhamish and Erzerum everything that was of value — small and heavy firearms, munitions, machinery from factories and laboratories, household furniture," etc.[3]

We find the following in still another communication:

"Those people who were saved from massacre are condemned to starvation and untold privation, since the districts of Kars and Alexan-

---

[1]Belleten, 1961, p. 489. See also Cebesoy, *Siyasi Ratilari,* "Vatan", Vol. III, No. 21 (1954).

[2]V. I. Lenin, *Doklad o vnutrennem i vnesnem polozenii Respubliki na Sovescanii aktiva Moskovskoj organizacii RKP(b) 9 oktjabrja 1920 goda.* "Leninskij sbornik", XXXVI (Moscow, Gospolitizdat, 1959), p. 131.

[3]CGAKA, f. 109, op. 3, d. 241, l. 12.

dropol are in total economic ruin. The Turks have taken out all the bread, rice, and other foodstuffs from these places. They have left behind not even one single animal, whether that be cow, horse, or sheep — all are headed in droves toward Erzerum. Parallel with this deathly economic breakdown are the relentless massacres which the Turks perpetrated in these same regions from the very first moment they invaded them. . . . The Armenian population of Alexandropol and of some tens of towns in various regions of Armenia have been put to the sword. . . ."[1]

In another document, a memorandum presented by Gosdanashvili to the ministry of foreign affairs of Soviet Georgia, we find described the Turkish occupation of Alexandropol:

"The Turks dismantled all telegraphic equipment, cut the city off from the world outside, and embarked on their monstrous plan — to exterminate a whole people. All roads leading from city to town, from town to city, were closed; they left nothing open. There was no food in the city. There was but one inference to be drawn from this: to starve the people to death. For the Turks the results were glittering: The impoverished inhabitants and the deported were dying in hundreds. Transportation facilities were inadequate to cope with the task of gathering the strewn corpses. . . . According to the figures of a committee formed by local authorities, the losses in life during the period of occupation of the city and the Alexandropol district are approximately as follows: Of the men, 30,000 were murdered, 20,000 were wounded, 16,000 were captives, and 10,000 died from hunger. Of the women, 15,000 were murdered, 5,000 were wounded, 3,000 were taken away as slaves, and 1,000 died from hunger. Of the children, 5,000 were murdered, 3,000 were wounded, and 10,000 died from starvation."[2]

In his telegram of June, 1921, to K. V. Tchicherin, the People's Commissar for Foreign Affairs of RSFSR, Alexander Miasnikian, President of the Council of People's Commissars of Soviet Armenia, informed him that, following the Turkish evacuation of Alexandropol, thousands of corpses of women and children were discovered in that city's environs.

"The investigating committee has just completed its work, the results of which we report to you for your information. . . ." Then the telegram went on to say: "The committee has counted 12,050 dead bodies in the districts of Aghpoulagh and Tchatchour, of which 80 percent are children of ages 5 to 12. There are numberless corpses of young women and girls." In a summary statement at the end, it said that, on the basis of the findings of the Alexandropol commit-

[1]*Ibid.*, d. 241, f. 12.
[2]*Politarxiv MID SSSR.*, inv. No. 53351, l. 14.

tee, the total number killed by the Turks reached 60,000, of which 30,000 were men, 15,000 women, 5,000 children, and 10,000 young girls. Of the 38,000 wounded, 20,000 were men, 10,000 women, 5,000 young girls, and 3,000 children. Some 18,000 men were carried away as prisoners. Only 2,000 have survived; the rest have died either from starvation, exposure to the elements, or by the sword.[1]

We find the following in a report made by the committee of the district of Alexandropol on December 24, 1920, to the Commissar of Internal Affairs concerning the slaughter and pillage of towns and villages in the area by Turkish soldiers:

"Hitherto unseen and unheard-of crimes are being perpetrated in the rural district. . . . All the towns are plundered, there is nothing left behind — no livestock, no bread, no clothes, nor yet fuel. The streets of these towns are filled with dead bodies. This is nothing yet: All this becomes still more intolerable when the soldiers harass their prisoners and punish the people in more horrible ways. Not content with this, they seek more pleasure by subjecting them to a variety of tortures. They force parents to hand over to these executioners their eight-year-old daughters and 20 to 25 year-old sons. They rape the girls and murder the young men — all this in the presence of parents. This is the way they conducted themselves in all the towns. Young girls and women up to the age of 40 are snatched away — no one knows whereto, while men up to 45 years of age are murdered. These towns are depopulated. The situation has no precedent; it is beyond description."[2]

The hypocrisy, the mendacity, of Turkish writers about the alleged "peaceful" mission of Kemalist forces in Transcaucasia, and specially in Armenia, has deeper roots. Even in the Fall of 1920, when Turkish hordes were penetrating deep into the heart of Armenian territory, putting cities and towns to fire and sword, exterminating the innocent, law-abiding populace, the leaders of the "New Turkey" were proclaiming shamelessly that their bayonets did not signify oppression but liberation from the Dashnag yoke. On the eve of the Turkish attack Kiazim Karabekir made a special announcement to the people of Armenia in which he proclaimed: "The purpose of the Kemalist attack is to liberate at once both the Christians and the Mohammedan population from the Dashnags."[3] And from Tiflis, the representative of the Ankara government, Kiazim Bey, had the gall to announce, after the Turk-

---

[1]*Arxiv vnesnej politiki SSSR*, f. 132, op. 4, p. 6, d. 14, 1. 52.

[2]*The Great Socialist October Revolution and the Victory of the Soviet Order in Armenia*, etc., *supra*, pp. 447–448. (In Armenian)

[3]*Central 'nyj partarxiv IML pri CK KPSS* f. 85, op. 14, d. 21, 1. 1.

ish forces had destroyed and pillaged occupied areas and exterminated the inhabitants:

"We are far removed from any intention to destroy Armenia, but wish for an Armenia that is democratically self-governed. Armenia herself can testify to the fact that not even a single oppressive act has been committed by us in the occupied areas."[1]

The appeal to world sentiment by the "Anatolia Agency" on October 23, 1920, was a good example of the fanatical and demagogic public pronouncements of the Kemalists. In this "document", written in French and sent out on behalf of the Ankara Government, Kemalists proferred "explanations" concerning "the clashes between Turkish nationalist forces and *Armenian gangsters* in the Caucasus".[2] (Italics ours.) Deliberately distorting the actual picture of things, the Kemalist government produced "official" statistical data in this "appeal", regarding the "cruelties" perpetrated by Armenians against the Mohammedan population in Kars and other areas, "the burning of 199 towns", etc. At the end of this entirely fraudulent declaration the Ankara Government attempted to convince world opinion that "the responsibility for the shedding of blood rests solely upon the Armenians".[3]

At the same time, Kemalists tried to hide their aggressive policy in Transcaucasia by symbolizing it as the struggle for Turkish independence against the Entente, which was a widely entertained sentiment during that period among the masses. A. B. Kadishchev's appraisal in his *Intervention and Civil War in Transcaucasia* is correct, when he says:

"They represented the war against Armenia as a fight against the Entente, which supplied them the opportunity to conceal their aggressive intentions in Transcaucasia."[4]

The aims of that attack were far from what Turkish propaganda presented them as being!

Dashnag detachments undertook on September 24, 1920, to clear the district of Olthie of Turkish forces. It must be noted that the Brest-Litovsk agreement* had, along with other territories,

---

[1]*Ibid.*, d. 21, l. 5.

[2]See *Arm. SSR Historical Archives,* f. 200, op. 1, d. 867, l. 40. (In Armenian)

[3]*Ibid.*, f. 200, op. 1, d. 867, l. 41.

[4]A. B. Kadishchev, *Intervencija i grazdanskaja vojna v Zakavkaz's,* p. 321.

*Peace Treaty signed on March 3, 1918, by Russia and Germany and her allies. (E.B.C.)

handed that district over to the Turks also. But the government of RSFSR had declared this predatory agreement void in a note dated September 20, 1918, in which it accused the Turkish Government of flagrant violation of Article Four of that Treaty, the provision that the future of the districts of Kars, Ardahan, and Batum, once parts of the Russian Republic, was to be decided by a free vote of their inhabitants. "Instead," the note charged, "following the signing of the treaty these areas were seized by Turkish armed forces and a military occupational regime established therein, accompanied by intolerable plundering and oppression of the civil-peaceful population. . . ." It then exposed the methods employed by Turkish authorities in conducting the so-called "plebiscite": That the people of these districts were so terrorized in advance and put in such a predicament as to make the right to self-determination reserved for them a shameful joke. That on the eve of election day, all citizens who enjoyed any reputation in these areas were either exiled or arrested, many of whom were even shot to death. That since the election was conducted under the direct control of Turkish authorities, it was not difficult to determine in advance what the outcome would be under the given circumstances.

Having construed the oppressive measures against the population of those districts snatched from Russia as a violation of Article Four of the Brest-Litovsk Treaty, the Soviet Government declared that:

> It cannot "accept the so-called expression of the will of the people in the districts of Kars, Ardahan and Batum; that it holds that the right of the people in these districts to found a new order has not been effected; that, therefore, the question of a new status is still unresolved."[1]

Although the Government of Soviet Russia had declared the Brest-Litovsk Treaty nugatory, making it obligatory for the Ankara Government, therefore, to evacuate its forces from the district of Olthie, the latter was in no way disposed to recognize the rights of Armenia to the territory involved. In point of fact, it had been looking for an excuse for aggressive action. For, from the very beginning Kemalist rulers made their position very clear toward the Brest-Litovsk Treaty. Thus, on April 23, 1920, the first day of the Grand National Assembly, Mustafa Kemal declared unequivocally in his address that "the boundaries of Turkey must include *Batum, Kars, Ardahan* in the Caucasus, and Mosul and Diarbekir in Mesapotamia".[2] (Italics ours.)

---

[1]*Dokumenty vnesnej politicki SSSR*, Vol. I, pp. 490–491.
[2]Gazata *Gruzija*, 1920, no. 89.

To retain possession of Olthie, the Kemalists undertook "to establish *de jure*" their "rightful" claim to the area on the basis of the predatory treaties of Brest-Litovsk and of Batum. This is what we read in a note sent by Ankara on July 8, 1920, to the Dashnag Government of Armenia:

> "As you also well know, the Brest-Litovsk Treaty, by which the Armenian Republic was formally recognized, and the Batum Treaty,* which supplements it, serve as the basis for the existing relations between the two Governments. These treaties are signed by fully empowered representatives, and approved and confirmed by both Governments. Since the Olthie district is included within the three vilayets (Kars, Ardahan, and Batum — the authors), under the terms of the aforementioned treaties, *in compliance with the free vote of the people,* it becomes the absolute possession of the Ottoman State."[1] (Italics ours.)

As to how popular and free was the "free" "plebiscite" administered by the Sultan's Government in 1918 was demonstrated above. Even the French newspaper *Le Bosphore,* of Istanbul, made note of the fact that if Enver annexed the provinces of Kars and Ardahan under the pretext of a "plebiscite" conducted by him, Kemal did not even do that. It wrote:

> "Mustafa Kemal demands that the Armenians acknowledge the pact of Brest-Litovsk, that is to say, they agree to cede the provinces of Kars and Ardahan to the Kemalists, which had earlier been occupied by Enver. And they ask this even though the same pact speaks of a prior plebiscite. . . ."[2]

The Dashnag Government in its reply of July 28 pointed out, however, that the arguments presented by the Ankara Government in its memorandum of July 8 were groundless, since the Treaties of Brest-Litovsk and Batum were signed by the Sultan's Government, which Kemalists do not recognize. It stated further on:

> "The fact that You accept as premise the Treaties of Brest-Litovsk and Batum, which basically do not acknowledge the actual existence of Armenia, deprives us, very much to our pain, of any hope of reaching an understanding with You, since You continue still to be

---

[1] *Arm. SSR Historical Archives,* f. 200, d. 402, l. 18.

[2] *Bjulleten Narodnogo Komissariata inostrannyx del RSFSR,* 1921, No. 57, p. 16.

*Signed by the Armenian Republic under duress on June 14, 1918, only seven days after its forced declaration of independence following the collapse of the Transcaucasian Seym (Federation). Georgia and Azerbaijan had declared their independence on May 26 and 27, respectively. (E.B.C.)

dominated by the aims and tendencies of the German Kaiser's and the Sultan's imperialist governments, which have found expression in those Treaties . . ." At the end, the note adds: "Armenia has no intention of making any moves beyond the former Turko-Russian borders. What is of special import is that it has the right to hope that Turkey shall not interfere in any issue that involves Armenian internal affairs. Consequently, Your demand to evacuate the district of Olthie, which forms an integral and undisputable part of the Republic of Armenia, and the aggressive movements of your soldiers in the same district are entirely inconceivable and unpermissible."[1]

The Bulletin of the Ministry of Foreign Affairs of the RSFSR states that "this terminated negotiations, and Kemalists began intensive preparations for an attack."[2]

There are documentary materials of special interest in the Armenian SSR Central Historical Archives relative to Kemalist military maneuvers and preparations, in one of which we read:

"1. Regiments (17, 28, 29, and 36) of the 15th Army stationed along the border were concentrated in the district of Bartous and Olthie. A general call to arms of men up to 40 was made. Harsh measures were taken against desertion. They succeeded fully in supplying each of these regiments with 1000 to 1100 bayonets — a total of 4000 to 4500.

"2. They organized two local companies, 2000 fighters, from among the Mohammedans of the district of Tortoum and Nariman.

"3. They sent agitators and spies into the district of Olthie among Kurds and Turks, who succeeded in organizing in northern sections of the district a number of *chetehs,* a total of close to 1000 'irregulars'.

"Finally, to reinforce this body of armed might they dispatched from Erzerum to Bartous as many as 400 gendarmes.

"Thus in this way the Turks were able to bring together, in the Bartous and Olthie district alone, up to 4500 regular soldiers and 3000 to 3500 irregulars."[3]

Mustafa Kemal himself acknowledges that they resolved for the second time to attack Armenia in September:

"We decided at that time to launch an attack on Armenia. We were busy with preliminary preparations. The necessary orders and instructions had been given to the commander of the Eastern front."[4] (Italics ours.)

---

[1]*Arm. SSR Historical Archives,* f. 200, op. 1, d. 402, l. 19. See also *Bjulleten Narodnogo,* etc. As above, pp. 16–17.

[2]*Bjulleten* . . ., as above, p. 17.

[3]*Arm. SSR Historical Archives,* f. 200, op. 1, d. 867, l. 19.

[4]Mustafa Kemal, *Put novoj Turcii,* Vol. III, p. 108.

The French newspaper, *Le Journal d'Orient*, in an article entitled, *How Kemalists Decided to Attack Armenia*, published on October 19, 1920, exposed the plans for attack by Kemalists, from which we quote in part:

"In search of some sensationalistically adventurous action, which they could exploit to boost the demoralized spirit of the population of Anatolia, Kemalists in Ankara conceived the project of a general attack on Armenia under the personal sponsorship of Mustafa Kemal himself, about which governmental bodies in Constantinople were undoubtedly informed in advance. Except that those in Constantinople did not know what kind of preliminary preparations predated this sudden decision. On September 7, the commander of the 15th Regiment, Kiazim Karabekir, arrived in Ankara from Erzerum, where on the very next day a meeting of the Supreme Military Council was called under the presidency of Mustafa Kemal. Attending the meetings were Generals Ahmed Fevzin, Mouhaetten, Ali Fuat and Nourettin, and Colonel Ismet Bey, Chief of the General Staff.

"General Kiazim Karabekir declared that a *general attack on Armenia was a must* . . .

"The Council then asked him if his forces were adequate, and if he was confident of total victory for Kemalist arms.

"Kiazim Karabekir answered that he has under him four divisions, two of which are under the command of Remzie.

"Each of these divisions numbered 8- to 9,000 men and would receive the aid of Turkish and Kurdish irregular forces. Although Turkish artillery at the Moslem front was still disorganized, according to Kiazim, it was nevertheless adequate.

"Now there was only one question that still remained unanswered for Mustafa Kemal, that is, the position of Georgia, in the event of an attack on Armenia, which was known to have an army that, however small in number, was very well organized."[1] (Italics ours.)

The same article then states that a secret delegation, headed by Yusouf Kemal Bey, was sent to Tiflis, where it met with Geordania, the president of the Supreme Council of Georgia, and Keketchgorie, Minister of Foreign Affairs, and received their assurances that "in the event of a Kemalist-Armenian conflict, Georgia will declare its strict neutrality. . . ."[2]

Whereupon the Kemalist army took advantage of events in the district of Olthie to launch its attack.

It should be noted that contemporary Turkish writers not only

[1]*Le journal d'Orient*, no. 704, October 19, 1920. (See Arm. SSR Historical Archives, f. 200, op. 1, d. 443, l. 36–37.
[2]*Ibid.*

openly write about the previously planned invasion of Armenia but
also acknowledge the fact that Kemalist forces started the military
operations. This is what Professor Enver Ziya Karal, for instance,
says in *The New Turkey,* published recently: "Our invasion movement of September 24, 1920, against Armenia ended in our decisive
victory."[1] Professor Ahmed Shoukrou Esmer writes the same thing
in his lengthy article, *Turkish Diplomacy during 1920–55,* which
appears in the same work.[2]

When it embarked on its already well-planned invasion, the
Ankara Government took stock also of the fact that Soviet Russia
was occupied with a war against Polish interventionists and that it
had transferred a number of divisions of its forces in the Caucasus
to the Polish front. Thus the Turkish rulers found conditions that
prevailed at the time favorable for embarking upon their aggressive
program — to put an end to Armenia as a sovereign state and to
place Soviet Russia before an accomplished fact.

Furthermore, they had still other motives behind this invasion.
By subjugating Eastern Armenia, they wished to demonstrate the
absolute inapplicability of the Sèvres Treaty* and thereby influence as well the policy of the Allied Powers toward Turkey. Concerning this intention of the Turkish Government *The London
Times* of December 22, 1920, says:

". . . Mustafa Kemal invaded Armenia in order to occupy Kars
and Ardahan. It occurs to him that by conquering Armenia, he shall
be able to exert pressure upon the Entente and America."[3]

Turkish forces were able to occupy a major portion of Arme-

---

[1]H. R. Ertug, *et al., Yeni Turkiye* (Istanbul, 1959), p. 58.
[2]*Ibid.,* p. 69.
[3]*Bjulleten Narodnogo,* etc., 1920, No. 25, p. 36. (Trans. from the
Armenian. E.B.C.)
*The peace treaty with Turkey, signed August 10, 1920, by repre-
sentatives of the Sultan, the Allied Powers, and the Armenian Republic,
which was recognized by all signatory powers. Turkey also agreed to the
extension of the boundaries of the Armenian Republic to include territories in Turkish Armenia. The task of drawing up the map of a united and
free Armenia was entrusted to President Wilson who, on November 22,
1920, awarded to the Armenian Republic some 40,000 square miles, com-
prising the stipulated Armenian provinces of Erzerum, Trebizond, Van,
and Bitlis. This boundary decision was binding on all signatory powers.
These and other historically Armenian territories, such as, Kars and Ardahan, are still part of Turkey. The Sèvres instrument was formally buried
by the Treaty of Lausanne, signed by Kemalist Turkey and the Allied
Powers on July 24, 1923. . . . The U. S. Senate rejected it in 1927. (E.B.C.)

nia in a very short time after the invasion. Soviet Russia once again attempted to intervene to put an end to that ludicrous war, and to save Armenia from total destruction. The Soviet Government of Russia was even ready to give military aid to Armenia. This is borne out by a statement made by LeGrand, representative of the RSFSR, to the Dashnag Government, on November 19, 1920, that if the Armenian Government were to seek military aid from Soviet Russia, that it would be given; that Soviet Russia could not remain indifferent to the Kemalist invasion, since

"that aggression has begun to take on a *purely imperialistic character.* The fulfillment of such Turkish aims would thereby bring about the strengthening of the imperialist predilections of Kemalists, which in turn would change the original nature of that movement as a liberationist movement. For Armenia to have Kars would not transform Armenia into an imperialistic country; whereas, if it were in Turkey's possession, in the event of changes in the disposition of Kemalists, it could play that very role. It is entirely obvious that the creation of such a change in character would present a decided threat to Russia, and that is contrary to the interests of Soviet Russia."[1]

During that same discussion, LeGrand turns to the question of military aid to Armenia and states definitely that, as a result of the victory over Wrangel and the liquidation of the Polish front, Soviet Russia possesses sufficient available forces which it is ready to employ immediately to prevent the Kemalist advance and thus free Armenia's territory of Turkish occupation.[2]

V. I. Lenin discusses this question in detail in his well-known address, *On Our Internal and External State and the Problems of the Party,* delivered on November 21, 1920, before the Moscow regional convention of the RC(b)P, in which he says:

"Developments in the Caucasus at the present time are very complicated and extremely difficult to appraise. We may, therefore, be engulfed in war any day. But such a war should not be terrifying now, in view of the almost completed settlement with Poland and the total liquidation of Wrangel. If such a war is hoisted on us, then that would mean for us *still more strengthening of our forces and of our position.* . . . We can look upon such a turn of events calmly, for it will be a war confined to a remote corner of the land. *This, in turn, will give our side perfect superiority of power, which probably will be* even more profitable for us than what we got from the Polish war."[3]

All this shows conclusively that Soviet Russia was favorably

---

[1] See *Arm. SSR Historical Archives,* f. 300, op. 1, d. 867, l. 332–333, 335–336.

[2] *Ibid.*

[3] V. I. Lenin, *Works,* Vol. 31, p. 520.

disposed toward, and was capable of rendering military assistance to, Armenia, even at the risk of war with Turkey.[1] Had the Dashnag government agreed to accept that assistance, the Armenian people would have avoided additional sacrifices of tens of thousands of lives and new territorial losses. However, the Dashnags preferred to come to an agreement with the Turkish plunderers, hoping thereby to prolong their rule a little longer with the help of the latter.

The Turkish invasion of 1920 ended with the defeat of the Dashnags and the signing of the crushing treaty of Alexandropol. Following the footsteps of Kemal[2], Turkish writers speak of it with special pride and bluster as "the first international agreement of the new Turkish state"[3], concealing from their readers the fact that, since that treaty was signed by a government that had been already overthrown, it had no *de jure* status. Nor do they tell them that the Turks failed to enforce the predatory terms of that treaty because of the establishment of a Soviet regime in Armenia and of the firm stand taken by Soviet Russia. As a result, the Treaty of Alexandropol* was not recognized either by Soviet Armenia or by Soviet Russia, and, along with the agreements of Moscow and Kars, was declared void by them.

---

[1]We deem it necessary to call attention to the fact that many of our historians unduly overemphasize the danger of the possibility of the Entente taking advantage of the Kemalists to promote their anti-Soviet policy. They represent the situation as if Soviet Russia was fearful of such an eventuality; that, in order to forestall it, it was, therefore, constrained to make major concessions. Such a viewpoint has no basis in fact whatever. In truth, the newly-created Soviet Republic had been able to turn back the invasion by fourteen nations, organized by the Entente, and to come out the victor in that unequal struggle. Furthermore, at the time when Kemalists invaded Transcaucasia, Soviet Russia had already completed the crushing of the interventionists and the internal anti-revolutionary elements. On the other hand, England, the power that inspired the Entente, having taken stock of the real situation, was engaged in negotiating with *RSFSR* for a trade agreement, and signed that pact on the very same day that the Turco-Soviet agreement was signed, namely, on March 16, 1921.

[2]Mustafa Kemal, *op. cit.,* Vol. III, p. 119.

[3]Prof. Dr. Ahmet Sukru Esmer, *Turk Diplomasisi,* 1920–1955, in "Yeni Turkiye" (Istanbul, 1959), p. 69.

*Negotiations for the armistice treaty of December 2, 1920, to end the disastrous Turco-Armenian war, began in September; Kiazim Karabekir's forces were now pounding at the very gates of Erevan.

In point of fact, this treaty was invalid since the Dashnag Government was not in existence, *de facto* or *de jure,* at the time of signing. It

Yet, Turkish writers falsely claim that Soviet Russia did recognize the Alexandropol Treaty. "According to the instrument signed on March 16, 1921", writes Professor Karal, "the Moscow government did recognize the agreement the Armenians signed with us."[1] (Reference is to the Alexandropol Treaty—authors.) Tevfik Biyiklioglu asserts that the present boundaries between Turkey and the Soviet Union were drawn by the treaties of *Alexandropol,* Moscow and Kars.[2] Unal's statement repeats the same refrain: "The Treaty of Kiumrie* was followed by those of Moscow and Kars."[3] But there is more to come! With shameless disregard for truth, and with intent to cover up the predatory character of the Alexandropol Treaty, this same author attempts this lame justification:

"The Armenians were compelled by the Kiumrie Treaty to resign for our benefit *from those territories of ours* lost by the Ottoman Empire in 1878."[4] (Italics ours.) According to him, by the terms of the Alexandropol Treaty Turkey was to receive back those territories, namely, Kars and Ardahan, which were annexed to Russia by the Treaty of Berlin in 1878. This is an absolute falsehood. First, because those lands are *historically* integral parts of Armenia, lands which Turks falsely identify as theirs originally.[5] Second, because Turkey grabbed not only those Armenian territories by the Treaty of Alexandropol but also others that are parts of Eastern Armenia.

We now see that Turkish historians, along with their justifying Turkish aggression against Armenia, "legalize" as well "a portion" of the results of that aggression — the predatory Treaty of Alexan-

---

[1]Prof. Enver Ziya Karal, *Birinci Cihan harbinden Lozan muahedesine Kadar Turkiyenin siyasi olaylari,* "Yeni Turkiye" (Istanbul, 1959), p. 58.

[2]See his *Ataturk Anadoluda,* p. 76.

[3]Tahsin Unal, *1700 den 1958 e Kadar Turk Siyasi Tarih* (Ankara, 1958), p. 270.

[4]*Ibid.*

[5]See also *Belleten,* Temmuz 1961, p. 487.

*i.e., Alexandropol, now Leninakan, second largest metropolis in Soviet Armenia. (E.B.C.)

---

had, in an extraordinary assembly during November 30 to December 1, 1920, attended as well by other Dashnag leaders, voted preference for Russian over Turkish orientation, declared Armenia a Socialist Republic on December 1, relinquished the reins of government to the Bolsheviks, and signed an agreement with the Soviets some time prior to the signing of the treaty with the Turks, whereby among other concessions, Armenian signatories relinquished rights in Turkish Armenia provided by the Treaty of Sèvres. For other details, see text. (E.B.C.)

dropol, by which the territory of Armenia was limited to the districts of Erevan and Lake Sevan, which in point of fact should have been subjected as well to Turkish domination! According to Article Two of the Treaty of Alexandropol the districts of Nakhitchevan, Sharour and Shahtakhtie were specifically put under Turkish rule. Turkey was given the right "to supervise the railroads and other means of transportation" (Article Eleven), "to undertake military measures in the territory of Armenia", and so on.[1] As it is justly remarked, in the *Soviet Historical Encyclopedia,* "By the Treaty of Alexandropol Armenia in essence became a vilayet [province] of Turkey."[2]

Turkish falsifications of historical fact and of documentary evidence have reached such heights as to claim that their aggressive operations and the subjugation of others' lands have been "contributions" to the victory of the Soviet order in Transcaucasia. We thus find Tevfik Biyiklioglu writing in the July, 1961, issue of the *Bulletin,* published by The Historical Society of Turkey:

> "During the time when Soviet Russia was extremely preoccupied with internal clashes and the war with Poland, its forces in Transcaucasia — in Azerbaijan, Armenia, and Georgia, were weak and disorganized. And the sovietization of those states and peoples was made *possible by virtue of Turkish assistance only."*[3] (Italics ours.)

But, what was that "assistance" rendered by Kemalist Turkey? Was it that the Turkish invasion of Transcaucasia had caused the Armenian people still more untold catastrophes and sacrifices? Was that "assistance" in the form of destruction of Armenian lives and property? For it is reported in *The Soviet Historical Encyclopedia* that:

> "on the basis of incomplete data the number of victims in just the areas occupied by the Turks, as a result of the Turco-Armenian war, was close to 198,000 lives, [and] the value of the properties destroyed and appropriated by the Turks is estimated at eighteen million gold rubles."[4]

Actually, Kemalists continued their predatory policy in Transcaucasia after the establishment of the Soviet system in Armenia, at the same time revealing clearly their anti-Soviet attitude. If

---

[1]Prof. Ju. V. Kljuchnikov and Prof. A. V. Sabanin, *Mezhdunarodnaja politika novejshego vremeni v dogovorax, notay i diklaracijay,* Part III, no. 2 (Moscow, 1929), pp. 71–73.

[2]*Sovetskaja istoricheskaja enciklopedia,* Vol. I (Moscow, 1961), p. 748.

[3]*Belletin,* Temmuz 1961, p. 488. See also the same author's *Ataturk Anadoluda,* pp. 19–20.

[4]*Supra.* Vol. I, p. 748.

Kemalist leaders were declaring demagogically on the eve of their invasion of Armenia that their attack of "short duration" had as its aim the liberation of the working masses of Armenia from the Dashnag yoke, they still continued to pursue the same policy against Armenia after its sovietization, as they had against Armenia ruled by the Dashnag party.

The overthrow of Dashnag rule and the sovietization of Armenia brought about radical changes in Transcaucasia, thereby creating a real opportunity to effect a just and durable peace between Kemalist Turkey and Soviet Armenia. The spirit of the new Armenia was expressed by the Military — Revolutionary Committee's declaration, of November 29, 1920, proclaiming the founding of the Armenian Socialist Soviet Republic. That statement said in part:

> "We believe the Turkey that is freed of its imperialistic yoke will extend a fraternal hand to us, now that we have vanquished our enemy and are together engaged in battle against the ravenous Entente. We are also convinced that it will not be the victor's sword that will suggest the conditions for the conciliation to come between Soviet Armenia and the workingman's Turkey, but the fraternal geniality and cooperativeness of the free peoples of Soviet Armenia and the workingman's Turkey."[1]

Let us now see how Kemalist Turkey treated Armenia after its sovietization.

With no consideration whatever of the new established order, the Ankara Government undertook to put into effect the enslaving provisions of the Treaty of Alexandropol. The Soviet Government of Armenia, in a memorandum on December 10, 1920, to Ahmed Moukhdar, Minister of Foreign Affairs of Turkey, said that it expected of the Ankara Government to declare void the peace treaty signed with the Dashnags, and agree to calling a conference soon,

> "to come to an understanding in the light of the new conditions consequent upon the revolutionary changes. The Soviet Government, therefore, considers that very necessary, since it has in its possession abundant information which, notwithstanding the new turn of events, definitely points to kinds of activities in the areas occupied by the Turkish military command, that cannot be explained in any other way than that the hostile, implacable policy toward Armenia is still being pursued. . . ."[2]

---

[1] *The Great Socialist Revolution of October and the Victory of the Soviet Order in Armenia*, p. 405. (In Arm.)

[2] *Documenty vneshnej politiki SSSR*, Vol. III, (Moscow, Gospolitizdat, 1959, p. 379.

The Ankara Government's note of December 15, 1920, not only indicated that Turkey was unwilling to give up the Treaty of Alexandropol, but it endeavored to "establish" its rights to the seized Armenian territories.

"The Turco–Armenian Treaty," it declared disdainfully, "is an agreement that is not based on force, but *on the right of self-determination of nations,* and we desire to annex *only territories with Turkish populations*."[1] (Italics ours.)

And in its memorandum of February 5, 1921, the Ankara Government further asserted that "the Treaty of Alexandropol does not represent force, but justice, the carrying out of which is a prerequisite to establishing peace in the Caucasus". With crude misrepresentation of actual conditions, the Kemalist Government insisted in the same note that "the areas ceded to Turkey were populated mainly by Turks."[2]

Thus, with utter disregard of the fact that a new, a Soviet, regime now existed in Armenia, and of the new Government's declaration of principles concerning foreign policy, which were proposed as the basis for a discussion of the problems of determining mutual friendly relations and of establishing a just peace, the Kemalist Government continued its aggressive operations against the Armenian people. And, if it had not been for the Government of Soviet Russia, the Armenian people would have been subjected to further sufferings and privations by Kemalist occupation forces.

The government of the RSFSR declared unequivocally that it did not recognize the predacious Treaty of Alexandropol. In his telegram of December 11, 1920, to K. G. Ortchoniktze, member of the Military-Revolutionary Council of the Caucasian theatre of war, Tchicherin proposed that the Turks be made to understand that the Soviet Government demands "the clearing of the Alexandropol district and the withdrawal from the province of Kars of Turkish soldiers."[3] Furthermore, Tchicherin sent a note directly to Turkey's Grand National Assembly on December 19, in which he said that, in order to demonstrate its feelings of cordiality towards the Soviet Government, as well as toward the workers and farmers of Armenia and all Soviet Republics, the Ankara Government

"should take the necessary steps so that the Turkish army may clear without delay the province of Alexandropol and all areas to the

[1] *Ibid.,* p. 397.
[2] *Ibid.,* pp. 487–488.
[3] *Ibid.,* p. 380.

north and east of the province of Kars, the occupation of which . . .
must not determine in advance the Turco-Armenian boundary line."[1]

In still another telegram sent to Ortchonikze on January 18,
1921, Tchicherin reiterated this stand of the Soviet Government:
"Every task of each and every Soviet Republic is also our task, and
we cannot be faithful to ourselves if we looked upon the destruction of a brother Soviet Republic with indifference."[2] At the time
of the second conference, begun on February 26, 1921, in Moscow,
the delegation of the Ankara Government, taking advantage of the
overthrow for a brief period of the Soviet regime in Erevan by an
adventurous act of the Dashnags*, once again came forward with
the demand that the question of boundaries be settled in accord-
ance with the Treaties of Brest-Litovsk and Alexandropol. Furthermore, by exploiting the same temporary turn of events, the
Turks refused to negotiate with the representatives of Soviet
Armenia, which had been invited to join the conference.

The determined position taken by the Government of Soviet
Russia forced the Turkish delegation to resign from the Treaties
of Brest-Litovsk and Alexandropol. And on March 16, 1921, an
agreement was signed by RSFSR and Turkey, whereby Turkey
received a large portion of the areas its armies had occupied in
Transcaucasia. The ceded area was 24.997 sq. kilometers, with a
population of 572,000, which until 1914 was part of the Russian
Empire. (It involved the province of Kars, Gaghuzvan, Ardahan,
Arthvin, the southern sector of the province of Batum, and the
district of Sourmalu.)

As a result of the invasion of Transcaucasia in the years 1920
and 1921, the Kemalists succeeded in partly fulfilling their plans
for territorial aggrandizement which they had inherited from the
Turkey of the Sultans.

This is what the French language newspaper, *Le Bosphore*,
had to say again about the territorial usurpations of Kemalists:

"Mustafa Kemal can no longer pretend that he is protecting
exclusively Turkish territories. . . . Kemal is pursuing Enver's
policy."[3]

---

[1]*Ibid.*, p. 393.

[2]*Ibid.*, p. 479.

[3]See *Bjulleten Narodnogo Komissariata inostrannyx del RSFSR*, 1921,
No. 57, p. 16.

*Known as the February revolt, commenced on the 18th. The interim
Dashnag rule and the accompanying fratricidal carnage lasted well-nigh
forty-five days. (E.B.C.)

Even after these territorial concessions, the Kemalist government continued to retain its soldiers in the district of Alexandropol within the territory of Soviet Armenia, although it was obligated by the Moscow Treaty to withdraw them without delay.

Not until April 22, 1921, did the Turks leave Alexandropol and its environs, and this only after A. I. Gheker, Commander of the 11th Army, presented the following ultimatum to Karabekir on April 13, upon instructions from the Soviet Government:

"In order to prevent any unpleasant misunderstandings, which may come about presently . . . we request of you to take immediate steps to evacuate the province of Alexandropol and to withdraw the Turkish forces beyond the boundaries drawn by the Moscow Treaty. In case I am not advised by you as to the withdrawal of such armed forces, I shall be compelled to order the Red army into the area in question. Should this happen, I absolve myself of any and all responsibility for such consequences as may follow from such an action."[1]

In addition, Kemalists exploited the weaknesses of the Menshevik regime in Georgia*, and in conspiracy with native Mensheviks attempted to extend their territorial possession at the expense of that country also, by involving it in the anti-Soviet bloc, made up of all the anti-revolutionary, displaced governments of Transcaucasia.

On March 17, 1921, that is, on the very next day following the signing of the Treaty of Moscow, the Ankara forces, in clear violation of the territorial provisions of that Treaty, occupied Batum. Apropos of this action we find Kiazim Bey, the representative of the Ankara Government in Tiflis, Georgia, saying in his order:

"By decision of the Government of the Grand National Assembly of Turkey, based upon our national rights that are confirmed by duly signed treaties at various times, the region of Batum, the provinces of Aghalkalak and Aghaltzeka are being returned on this day to the folds of the Motherland, and, politically and administratively, will be subject to the Turkish National Government."[2]

It was only because of the speedy action taken by the 11th Army in Transcaucasia that these areas in Soviet Georgia were liberated from the Turkish usurpers. Red battalions entered Batum

---

[1]See *Bulletin (social sciences)*, Academy of Science of the Arm. SSSR, 1957, No. 2, pp. 97–98. (In Arm.)

[2]See *CGAOR Gruz. SSSR*, f. 13s, op. 1, ed. xr. 66, l. 33.

*Became a Soviet Republic on February 25, 1921. Azerbaijan's sovietization occurred on April 28, 1920. (E.B.C.)

on March 18, and on March 21 the last of the Turkish detachments laid down their arms, and surrendered.

It is these aggressive operations of the Kemalist regime in Transcaucasia which Turkish historians represent as "assistance" in the successful establishment of the Soviet order therein. . . .

7

EMERGENCE OF A MUTILATED ARMENIAN SSR
(1920–1921):

Just short of total annihilation! Rancor and machinations continue.

Young Turk - Kemalists

WE FIND THE HISTORY of events leading to the signing of the Treaties of Kars and Moscow also misrepresented in the works of contemporary Turkish historians. They accuse Soviet Russia for the delay in signing the 1921 Moscow pact. This is what Professor Ziya Karal is, in effect, saying:

"The Soviets were in no hurry to sign the 1921 treaty. They awaited developments to get a clear picture of the authority of the Grand National Assembly." In his opinion, the Moscow Treaty was signed "as a result of the victories over the Armenians in the East and over the Greeks in the West in the first battle at Inonou, as well as the invitation Turkey received from the Entente powers to the London Conference."[1]

Thus, according to Karal, it was under the compelling influences of these events that led Soviet Russia to sign the treaty of March 16, 1921. This twisting of the facts is actually intended to serve him so that he might represent the new state of things in the brightest colors: to picture the Turkey of the day as a very strong nation, with which the Great Powers of the West had to reckon, and, thus, to justify his rejecting the value of, and the need for, the Moscow Treaty for his country.

---

[1]Karal, *op. cit.,* p. 109.

Let us consider one by one the "facts" adduced by this historian: Was it Turkey's victory over Armenia, that was in virtual ruin under the Dashnag rule, which was the proof of the striking power of the Ankara government? Under the circumstances such a victory was not difficult of attainment, particularly when Kemalists had concentrated their main armed might, early in the Summer of 1920, against Armenia, as we have already pointed out. What about his other argument? Was it really the first battle (in January, 1921) at Inonou which decided the successful outcome of Turkey's national-liberationist movement? Turkish arms barely succeeded in staying the advance of the Greek army, and this with great difficulty. Nor did the Turks attempt to push forward. Even after that defeat, the Greeks represented a formidable force, had notable successes, and in August, 1921, were within range of Ankara. Now it is a fact that the Treaty of Moscow was signed six months before the Turkish army, commanded by Kemal, defeated the Greeks in September, 1921, in the battle of Sakaria. And it took another year to achieve a decisive victory over the Greeks near Domloupinar.

Although Karal mentions the London Conference, he does not say a word about its wretched failure. This meeting of the Allied powers during February and March, 1921, concerned itself also with the Near Eastern question with a view to re-considering the Treaty of Sèvres. Kemalists had entertained great hopes in connection with this conference; they thought that England was ready to make definite concessions. But the negotiations failed to give any aid or comfort whatsoever to Kemalists. The specific proposals of the Ankara delegation involving the revision of the Treaty of Sèvres — the re-establishment of the 1913 boundaries of Turkey in Europe, the evacuation of Greek forces from the Smyrna district, the fixing of boundaries with Armenia in compliance with the Treaty of Alexandropol — all these proposals the conservative *London Times* declared "ludicrous demands" on February 25, 1921. Subsequently, Kemal himself acknowledged that the Turkish delegation at the London Conference was convinced that, "The Entente nations wished to guarantee the unobstructed carrying out of the articles of the Treaty of Sèvres."[1]

During the Conference the leader of the Turkish delegation, Bekir Sami Bey, Minister of Foreign Affairs, carried on secret negotiations with Lloyd George, the Prime Minister of England. Sami Bey proposed Turkish membership in the anti-Soviet bloc of powers with a view to creating a buffer state between the West and

----

[1]M. Kemal, *Put 'novoj Turcii*, Vol. III, p. 200.

Soviet Russia by uniting with Turkey the mountaineers of northern Transcaucasia.[1] Because of the failure of the London Conference to promote the fulfillment of the national aims of Turkey and the disclosure of the fact of secret negotiations, the Ankara Government was forced to dismiss Sami Bey, as well as blamed him for the guilt in negotiating secretly with Lloyd George.

Thus, their ignominious failure at the London Conference, as well as the threats of a new attack by the Greeks, compelled Kemalists to approach the Turco-Soviet negotiations in Moscow at the time with more seriousness. It was after this change of attitude that an agreement was reached, and the signing of the Treaty on March 16 made possible.

Turkish historians deliberately pass over certain salient factors when they, wholly unjustifiably, blame the government of RSFSR for undue procrastination in reaching an agreement at Moscow. There is documentary evidence to prove that Soviet Russia had accepted in principle, as early as November, 1920, to call a conference in Moscow for a Turco-Soviet treaty. For instance, the meeting of the Political Bureau of the Central Committee of the RC(b)P on November 27, under the leadership of V. I. Lenin, having appraised prevailing conditions in Transcaucasia, decided that an immediate settlement of peace and order therein was an absolute necessity.[2] On December 1, 1920, Tchicherin telegraphed P. V. LeGrand, the representative of RSFSR in Armenia, instructing the latter to explain the position of his government on certain issues involving Transcaucasia.

"We wish to know", wrote Tchicherin, "if the Turkish Government has received the first draft[3] of the treaty, which we and Bekir Sami Bey prepared, and which was sent to Ankara with Yousuf Kemal. Does the Turkish Government consider it acceptable, and how does it feel about those matters which caused disagreement between us and Bekir Sami, and about which the latter could not come to any decision."[4]

And on December 9, 1920, the Government of the RSFSR in a memorandum, which welcomed the calling of a Turco-Soviet conference, stated that it was necessary to have representatives of

[1]See Halide Edib, *The Turkish Ordeal* (New York, London, 1928), p. 255.
[2]*Leninskij sbornik*, XXXVI, p. 144.
[3]This refers to the August 24 preliminary version of the Soviet-Turkish treaty signed by the conferees.
[4]*Dokumenty vneshnej politiki SSSR*, Vol. III, pp. 364–365.

Soviet Armenia and Azerbaijan present at this conference, since it must "decide on territorial and other issues involving those Governments and Turkey and Russia."[1]

Karal's 'exposition' of the reasons for the signing of the 1921 treaty is not unique. Altemur Kilic, equally guilty of distorting the course of events involved in Soviet-Turkish relations in his book published in the United States, in essence repeats the same falsehood, when he says:

"The 1921 treaty was signed only after the victories, first against the Armenians, then against the Greeks on the Western front, convinced the Soviet leaders that the star of Turkey was once more on the move."[2]

Similar misrepresentations are made in the treatments of the Treaty of Kars, signed on October 13, 1921, by Turkey and the Soviet Republics of Transcaucasia.

If Professor Karal attributes the delay in effecting an agreement at Moscow to the policy of Soviet Russia, on the other hand, Mukerrem Kamil Su and Kamil Su do the very same thing for the Treaty of Kars in their textbook, *The History of the Turkish Republic*, thus:

"Before the Russians came forward to act as mediator, they wished to determine the strength and power of the Turkish government. They, therefore, waited for a while. It was only after the great victory of the Turkish army near Sakaria that they acknowledged to themselves the strength of the new Turkish government, whereupon they mediated between us and the Caucasian Republics in the signing of the treaty."[3]

This deliberate falsification by Turkish writers, let us note, is "founded" on *Tarih (History)*, prepared by the Turkish Historical Commission, in which we read:

"The Moscow government delayed for a time the signing of the Treaty of Kars. It was only after the victory of the Turks on the Sakaria River that it signed that treaty."[4]

In point of historical fact it was Turkey which was responsible for the procrastination of negotiations, the delaying tactics employed, to reach an agreement with the Transcaucasian Republics.

---

[1]*Ibid.*, p. 371.

[2]Altemur Kilic, *Turkey and the World* (Washington, 1959), p. 39. (Trans. from the Arm. text. E.B.C.)

[3]*Türkiye Cumhuriyeti Tarihi* (Istanbul, 1957), p. 85.

[4]*Tarih*, Vol. IV, "Turkiye Cumhuriyeti" (Istanbul, 1934), pp. 103–104.

This is amply borne out both by source-materials found in archives, as well as by additional facts and documents brought to light in recent times.

The Treaty of Moscow of March 16, 1921, made provision for the signing of an agreement between Turkey and the Soviet Republics of Transcaucasia for the purpose of establishing orderly and normal relations between these states. But the Ankara government itself, under one pretext or another, repeatedly postponed those negotiations. And the basic reason for these postponements and delays was Turkey's unwillingness to resign from its determination to implement the predacious Treaty of Alexandropol, which the Moscow Treaty had declared null and void. This fact is made crystal-clear in Tchicherin's memorandum of April 8, 1921, to Ali Fuat, the Ambassador of Turkey in Moscow:

"I cannot conceal from you," wrote Tchicherin, "the great astonishment which I felt upon learning of the statement made by Kemal Fevzi Pasha, Minister of War in the Government of the Grand National Assembly of Turkey.

"The Minister of War declares in particular that the Turkish Army must remain on the Eastern front to serve the role of a balancing force. It is difficult for me to see what other military force it is intended to counteract, in order to sustain the balance of power in the Caucasus. Since the only other military power in that area is the Red army of the united Soviet Republics, the inference is drawn that, in the judgment of the Minister of War, the Turkish army must play a role inimical to Soviet forces and as a counterbalancing power against Soviet military might."

Whereupon the memorandum observes that the Minister's statement wholly contravenes the provisions of the Moscow Treaty, and constitutes a hostile act against Soviet arms. Referring to that portion of the declaration by Fevzi Pasha in which he had asserted that the evacuation of the territories of Armenia occupied by the Turkish army will be carried out only after the execution of the terms of the Alexandropol Treaty, the Government of Soviet Russia declared in no uncertain terms that it considers "the desire to put into effect the Treaty of Alexandropol as tantamount to abrogating the Treaty of Moscow'."[1]

Tchicherin in a telegram to K. G. Ortcheniktze instructed him to convey to the Ankara Government that it was necessary to effect without delay the new boundaries drawn by the Moscow Confer-

---

[1]*Documenty vneshnej politiki SSSR*, Vol. IV, pp. 53–54.

ence and to evacuate Alexandropol immediately of all Turkish
soldiers:

> "Convey strong objections in our name to Karabekir Pasha's
> declaration that he does not want to evacuate Alexandropol, and in-
> form as well the Government of the Grand National Assembly of our
> irrevocable insistence that the Turkish forces must withdraw with dis-
> patch beyond the boundary lines determined in Moscow. Point out
> the fatal consequences that may ensue from a clash between the forces
> of the Red Army and Turkish soldiers . . ." Once again the Govern-
> ment of RSFSR reminds the ruling circles in Ankara that "all Soviet
> Republics are closely tied to Soviet Russia with an inviolable pact."[1]

Even after these admonitions and reminders, the Turkish Government persisted in a devious and covert manner to hang on to
the Treaty of Alexandropol.

Representatives at the Moscow Conference had agreed that the
Turkish delegation would stop over at Tiflis, Georgia, to negotiate
a treaty with the three Republics in Transcaucasia. Yet upon their
arrival Yousuf Kemal, head of the delegation and Minister of Foreign Affairs, unexpectedly announced that he can only sign a treaty
with Georgia and Azerbaijan, and that he is not empowered to
carry on negotiations with Armenia. This is the reason, therefore,
the planned conference between the three Republics and Turkey
did not take place. Yet, the Ankara Government attempted to
hoist the responsibility for the failure on Soviet Russia and the
three Soviet Republics by accusing them of not honoring Article
15[2] of the Moscow Treaty. In his communication of June 6, 1921,
Tchicherin himself answered the charge that article 15 had not
been carried out only because the Turkish delegation had made it
impossible to negotiate a treaty between the Transcaucasian
Republics and Turkey.[3]

It was as late as June 14 when the People's Commissariat of
Foreign Affairs received word from Ali Fuad, the Turkish Ambassador, that his country agrees to negotiating a pact with all three
Republics of Transcaucasia. The delay of three more months
subsequently was also caused by the stand taken by Ankara.

Contrary to its original proposal to have the conference at

---

[1]*Ibid.*, p. 55.

[2]Article 15 obligated Soviet Russia to take the necessary steps to assure
the approval by the three Transcaucasian Republics of those Articles of this
Treaty that concerned them. See *Documenty vneshnej politiki SSSR*, Vol.
III, p. 602.

[3]*Op. cit.*, Vol. IV, p. 169.

Kars,[1] the Government of Turkey now suggested Ankara, which was altogether unsuitable for the Republics of Transcaucasia (because of the lack of facilities for the delegations to communicate with their respective governments). Tchicherin's reply of August 8, 1921, rejected that proposal, and gave the additional reason that Ankara was too close to the theater of war. Turkey insisted on its proposal once again, but to no avail.

These facts, therefore, clearly disprove the contentions of Turkish historians that the Soviets were responsible for the delays in negotiating the Treaty of Kars. What is more, because of the persistent attempts of the Kemalists to impose the Treaty of Alexandropol on Soviet Armenia, the RSFSR itself was specially interested in expediting an agreement between Turkey and the Transcaucasian Republics.

Turks resorted to similar delaying, dishonest tactics during the conference in Kars. A. Muravian, People's Commissar of Foreign Affairs of Soviet Armenia, reported on October 5, 1921, that "the Turks are deliberately stalling negotiations in the hope that the Polish-Russian crisis will become acute".[2] Y. Ganetzkin, the RSFSR representative, telegraphed Tchicherin on October 6:

> "All of us are left with the impression that the Turks are deliberately procrastinating at the Conference. News is circulating in the city that war will be declared against Poland any day now. It is definitely clear to all of us that the Turkish delegation is exploiting such an eventuality."[3]

Turkish historians have misrepresented, in their typical, fraudulent manner, the course negotiations at Kars took. Its impartial treatment will inevitably demonstrate that the Ankara Government is guilty of a dishonest and equivocal policy not only toward the Republics of Transcaucasia, but also toward Soviet Russia. Turkish historians say that nothing out of the ordinary happened at the Conference, that "the negotiations ran smoothly. . . ."[4] Yet, the materials found in archives, and, above all, the minutes of the sessions of the Conference clearly show that the negotiations had an extremely strained and intense quality, and this, because of the openly inimical attitude of the Turkish delegation toward Soviet Armenia.

---

[1]*Ibid.*, Vol. IV, pp. 227, 249, 255, 287.
[2]*Arm. SSR Central Historical Archives of the October Revolution and Socialist Reconstruction*, f. 40/113, op. 3, d. 75, l. 56. (In Arm.)
[3]*Ibid.*, f. 40/113, op. 3, d. 75, l. 50.
[4]Ali Fuat Cebesoy, *Moskova hatiralari* (Istanbul, 1955), p. 259.

The Turks raised the issue of independent treaties with individual Republics at this conference, too. They really wanted the chance to meet separately with the representatives of Soviet Armenia so that they could propose their terms, unhindered; that is to say, to impose on Armenia the plundering Treaty of Alexandropol. They brought up the question unexpectedly in the very first session; unexpectedly, because the proposal had been rejected before. But the united and determined stand of the three Republics caused the Turks to yield in the end. This is how G. C. Ordzonikidze describes the events revolving around this issue:

"Our delegation informed the Turks in no uncertain terms that it demands negotiations be conducted collectively with all Transcaucasian Republics and one treaty only be signed. . . . In response to the Turkish request for a legal justification of our proposal, we explained that the Transcaucasian delegation represented the Federation of the Transcaucasian Republics."[1]

But the Turks still persisted in their harassment, and in the September 30th session they asked the provocative question: "What is the nature of the interrelationships that exist between the Soviet Republics of Armenia, Georgia, and Azerbaijan?" Tchicherin gave a formal answer in his note of October 3 to the Turkish Minister of Foreign Affairs: That the Governments of the three Transcaucasian Republics had kept the Government of Soviet Russia informed of the existence of a political-economic agreement and of close ties between them, and that all their political and economic problems are resolved by them in unison.[2] Not until this action by Soviet Russia did the Turkish delegation (headed by that inveterate fanatic and executioner, Kiazim Karabekir Pasha) consent to negotiate a treaty collectively with the three Soviet Republics, namely, Armenia, Azerbaijan, and Georgia.

There was heated argument also about the disposition of large quantities of materials and equipments which the Turks had plundered and removed from occupied Alexandropol. The Transcaucasian delegation insisted on their replacement, while the Turks shamelessly attempted to "prove" their right to them.[3]

As to the question of a final rectification of Turco-Soviet boundaries, the Turkish delegation once more revealed its inflexibly hostile attitude towards Soviet Armenia. It is quite true

[1]G. K. Ordzonikidze, *Izbrannye stati i reci* (Moscow, 1939), p. 177.
[2]*Documenty vneshnej . . . (supra)*, Vol. IV, p. 392.
[3]See *Arm. SSR Central Historical Archives of the October Revolution and Socialist Reconstruction*, f. 40/113, op. 3, d. 75, l. 59.

that the Kars Conference did not concern itself with territorial questions as such, since these were taken up in the Treaty of Moscow. But the Transcaucasian delegation did come up with a proposal to revise the Soviet-Turkish boundary line slightly, namely, to transfer to Soviet Armenia the city of Ani with its historic ruins because of their unique value as monuments of the culture of the Armenian people. The Turks refused to comply, notwithstanding the fact that the Government at Ankara had earlier given its consent.[1]

8

PAN-TURKISM TODAY: Aims and Dangers

THE FOREGOING EXAMPLES of the pseudo-scientific treatment by modern Turkish historians of certain problems involving the not-too-distant past demonstrate the mendacious manner with which, among others, it serves the following objectives: On the one hand, their works attempt to justify the ultra-nationalistic, the fanatical and genocidal policy and activities of both the Sultan's Government and the leaders of the Young Turk party, and, on the other, their Pan-Turkist programme of aggressive maneuvering and of territorial aggrandizement at the expense of other peoples. Thus, they misrepresent the invasion of Transcaucasia in 1920–1921 as an integral part of the national-liberation struggle, and the areas annexed, as a result of that aggression, as traditionally, really Turkish lands.

Furthermore, there is a studied promotion of an anti-Soviet policy that is decidedly permeated with the spirit of Pan-Turkism. This reactionary ideology serves even today as an effective weapon of Turkish foreign policy in current schemes of political-nationalist expansion.

This contention is strikingly borne out by the so-called first Pan-Turkist Congress, which was held in Istanbul in March, 1955

---

[1]CGAOR Azerb. SSR, f. 4s/28r, op. 1, ed. xr., 81.

— with the full knowledge of the Turkish Government — and attended by invited repatriates and other "compatriots" in the diaspora. Those who spoke called for the extension of the frontiers of the Turkish world through "liberating Turkish brethren who live outside of Turkey". The congress took into this "Great Turkey" the Caucasus, the Middle East, Bovoldjie, and all those lands that are inhabited by Turkish-speaking peoples. Characteristically enough, participants in the congress elected Menderes, who was Prime Minister of Turkey at the time, as honorary president of their federation.[1]

Pan-Turkism is still a useful aggressive weapon in the armamentarium of Turkish reactionaries.

The extremely biased spirit and direction of Turkish historiography has, likewise, brought about an infiltration of militant Pan-Turkist ideas and feelings among large segments of the Turkish people, and, of consequence, hatred of racial minorities within the country, as well as of the peoples of neighboring states.

And its wide-spread pernicious influence has been a major stumbling block in the struggle of liberal and progressive elements against both foreign imperialists and native reactionaries, and for genuinely democratic and peace-promoting institutions in that country.

---

[1]*Protiv fal' sificacii istorii Vostoko* (Moscow, Izd. Vostochnoj Literatury, 1961), p. 98.

Some Salient Facts on Armenia

(EDITOR'S ADDENDUM)

The Armenian *SSR,* one of the fifteen Republics of the *USSR,* is confined to an area of 11,306 square miles, about 90% the size of Massachusetts and Connecticut combined. The pre-Soviet Republic of Armenia (1918–1920) in the Caucasus, prior to the invasion by Kemalist Turkey in 1920 and its subsequent dismemberment, is estimated at 26,491 square miles.

Historically, the Armenian homelands, in Turkey and the Soviet Union combined — extending from Transcaucasia to the Mediterranian Sea — and including such districts as Nakhitchevan, Zangezur, Karabagh, Akhalkalak, and, in Turkey, the vilayets, Van, Bitlis, Diarbakir, Harpout, Sivas, Erzerum, Trebizond, and Cilicia, represent some 130,000 square miles.

To the pre-Soviet Armenian Republic the Sèvres Treaty (August, 1920) added roughly 40,000 square miles by accepting the detailed demarcation of the south-western boundaries between Armenia and Turkey drawn by President Wilson (November 22, 1920) to whom this task was entrusted by the signatory powers. This "Wilsonian" Armenia in Turkey involved the Armenian vilayets of Bitlis, Van, Erzerum, and Trebizond. Combined with the then Armenian State, which still included Kars and Ardahan, it totalled about 67,000 square miles. . . .

In 1920, on the eve of its sovietization, Armenia's population was 780,000, swelled by refugees from Turkey. It was war-torn, poverty-stricken, and subject to epidemics. However, on January 1, 1964, it reached 2,070,000, over 90% of whom are Armenians. Intermittently since 1924, Soviet Armenia has also absorbed 200,000 repatriates, preponderantly from the Middle East, Greece, and Cyprus — one-time refugees or deportees from Turkey of the Young Turks and Kemalists. Since 1963, repatriation from the Middle East and Cyprus has been given impetus again.

In addition, around 900,000 Armenians live in the Soviet Republics of Georgia and Azerbaijan, almost equally divided between them. In Georgia, they are concentrated in Tiflis, its capital, which was one of the great centers earlier of Armenian intellectual life in the dispersion, and the Akhalkalak district adjacent to Armenia. In Azerbaijan, they are settled, for the most part, in Zankezur and the Karabagh *Oblast* (created in 1923) in the east, and in the autonomous Nakhitchevan district, which lies within Soviet Armenia and has, along the southeast, common boundaries with Turkey and Iran, but none with Azerbaijan itself. Nakhitchevan, predominently Armenian in culture and population (as are the other areas), was placed "under the protectorate of Azerbaijan, *provided Azerbaijan shall cede this protectorate to no other country*", by the Treaties of Moscow (Article 3), and Kars (Article 5) in 1921. . . . (My italics. See Map, p. 9).

With Armenians elsewhere in the Soviet Union, their total number well-nigh exceeds the three million mark.

Erevan, the one-time typical Asian town, now the capital of Armenia, is a metropolis "with wide thoroughfares, squares, parks, fountains and architectural ensembles". An ultra-modern cultural center, with a population of 600,000, it symbolizes a phenomenal, diversified, cultural growth — an unprecedented creative upsurge of the intellectual and spiritual forces at work in the entire country. It symbolizes the Armenian people's tremendous achievements in education on all levels; in the physical and human sciences; in literature, music and drama; in industry and technological know-how; and in architecture, sculpture and painting — however much still remains to be achieved. The singular accomplishments of individual scientists, *in Armenia itself,* as, for instance, in astrophysics, archaeology and biology, and of creative artists, as in music, painting and architecture, are well known, indeed, to the informed beyond the country's narrow confines.

One cannot help but contrast this picture — however invidious this sort of thing always is — with that presented by "modernized" Kemalist Turkey, as appraised by foreign writers, as well as by some enlightened Turks themselves who seem very much concerned over the still tragic state of cultural affairs of their country. Would that, of course, this were not so! For much more good could probably come from peoples when they are enlightened, culturally creative, and manifest a spirit of fair-play.